ONLINE MARKETING FOR BABY BOOMERS

and anyone else who doesn't speak geek

Fiona Blinco

Published by DIY Digital, Adelaide South Australia
diydigital.com.au

First edition 2020

Illustrations by Mike Tye

Some names and identifying details have been changed to protect the privacy of individual business owners.

DISCLAIMER
All information, techniques, skills and concepts contained within this publication are general in nature and are not given as individual advice. The intent is to offer a variety of information to provide a wide range of choices, recognising that we all have different circumstances and viewpoints. Should any reader choose to make use of the information contained herein, this is their decision, and the contributors (and their companies), author and publisher do not assume any responsibility whatsoever under any conditions or circumstances.

INTRODUCTION

Online Marketing, or Digital Marketing as it is also called, has well and truly come of age, and so have those of us who didn't grow up with computers. We went from manual typewriters to electric ones to desktops and now smartphones.

The Yellow Pages are no longer the viable alternative they once were. Promoting your business invariably requires consideration for your website, email marketing, Google presence and social media activity.

This book gives you guidance on whether to include, or eliminate, the most popular online marketing activities available to today's businesses and organisations.

Shining a light on the dark arts of digital marketing, this book is for business owners who want it spelt out simply and easily. With case studies and practical steps on what to do and what not to do, Fiona Blinco explains the main online marketing concepts small businesses and associations need to know to be successful.

It will help business owners and club volunteers start, or re-energise, their online marketing activities.

ENDORSEMENTS

"Fiona made the technology information I'm not used to, much simpler than what I expected. She has encouraged me to get my new business out there via some of her great suggestions."

Susie Dolling, Holistic Heart Healer

"As Fiona suggested, each time we hit between 250/300 visitors we get a sale! I had my first sale with Google as referrer the other day — which I was thrilled about! Visits are on the increase daily/monthly! Without Fiona's course I wouldn't have realised the importance of tracking this so carefully, and probably would have given up!"

Evanthe Dunn, Fave Jewellery, Etsy Seller

"It was a great experience meeting Fiona and thank you for all the valuable information and guidance....! You really make the complexities of digital marketing simple and professional through your awesome knowledge....!"

Renju Varghese, Inspired Digital Marketing

"Fantastic seminar on Facebook marketing. One tip alone added over 60 page likes in 24 hours."

Brett Jensen, Fleurieu Folk Festival

"Just attended the DIY Digital workshop on SEO and am much wiser. Thanks Fiona. The session was well run, highly informative with lots of practical advice for a small business owner like me."

Caroline Rowe, Author and Cook, Just4Me

ABOUT THE AUTHOR

Fiona has a Graduate Certificate in Social Entrepreneurship and Innovation and a Graduate Certificate in Business Administration. She has worked in national marketing roles in Australia for the Medic Alert Foundation, Whale and Dolphin Conservation Society and Multiple Sclerosis. She has 15 years' experience in fundraising and marketing in the not-for-profit sector in South Australia.

At 50 years old Fiona started her own business, DIY Digital. As a Gen X'er she has helped many of her own generation, plus plenty of Baby Boomers.

She manages several online marketing campaigns for clients as well as helping hundreds of small business owners navigate the myriad of digital marketing options through consultation sessions.

Fiona is passionate about the #shoplocal movement and regularly presents seminars and workshops on Google, Mailchimp and online marketing techniques. Keeping customers loyal and finding new ones through a savvy online presence is what she loves to do, and to share, with business owners.

> Fiona is available as a keynote speaker, panelist and for media appearances. For contact details and media resources visit the DIY Digital website at diydigital.com.au.

TABLE OF CONTENTS

CASE STUDIES

PROLOGUE

Remember playing Space Invaders at the local fish and chip shop? Remember going to the arcade with your friends and playing pinball, racing or shooting games? I sure do.

In offices, homes and classrooms electric typewriters started turning up, replacing the need for the clumsy Liquid Paper and Tippex correction fluid.

In schoolyards everywhere maths and computer geniuses were being ostracised as nerds, only to be, 20 years later, making more money than any of us could imagine.

The internet was in its infancy in the 1990s. We moved from faxing to emailing, we discovered how to text a message with our Nokia phone but landlines were still the norm for most of our communication.

Except for the very few early adopters and experimenters, those of us born before 1970 did not grow up with computers in our classrooms or our homes. Sometime in our early or mid-career they came along. Those who worked outside of the office environment, for example tradespeople, police officers and nurses, weren't introduced to the technology until much later. The initial transition for many of us was not smooth.

The Yellow Pages are no longer the viable alternative they once were. Promoting your business invariably requires consideration for your website, email marketing, Google presence and social media activity.

Online marketing, by its nature, uses online tools and platforms. Being comfortable and confident in using the technology is a must.

Understanding how digital marketing strategies work, and when and where to use them, are an essential part of today's toolkit for businesses. Whether it's being able to better understand the language and delivery of services provided by professionals or attempting to do-it-yourself, keeping up-to-date is imperative.

This book presents an overall view of the main online tools you need to consider in order to either include them, or eliminate them, in the digital marketing strategy for your business.

THE BIGGER PICTURE

CHAPTER 1

DIGITAL MARKETING STRATEGY

Not that long ago, for many small businesses and sole traders, marketing a business was centred around putting an advert in the Yellow Pages. You'd get a phone call once a year to remind you the advert was due for renewal. They'd fax you the artwork, you'd scrawl any changes you wanted on the paper and fax it back. Easy wasn't it?

Marketing used to be easy. It wasn't necessarily cheap – but it was easy.

With everyone using the internet to find things, marketing has become complicated. A lot of it is very cheap, if you know how to use it, but for many of us it isn't easy – especially for those of us who are not digital natives.

There are so many things a business could be doing to promote itself online it's hard to work out which marketing strategy will work. Even if you know what your ideal strategy is, you've then got to work out how to do it.

There are certain digital marketing activities that tend to suit one business type or sector over another – but as with all marketing – there are rarely guarantees. Sometimes going with an unlikely strategy can put you ahead of, or at least in a different place, to your competitors.

There are six online marketing activities we'll be looking at in this book. By considering each of these six main activities you can then eliminate them, or include them, in the marketing strategy for your business.

1. Website
2. Search Engine Optimisation
3. Google Advertising
4. Social Media
5. Facebook Advertising
6. Email Marketing

Website

Having a website is a must for pretty much all businesses.

Some sole traders start out with a Facebook page and feel this is enough – but a Facebook page on its own will make the business look like a hobby rather than a serious business.

Some baby boomer business owners refer to their Facebook page as their website – as if it is the same thing – it isn't. A website is different from a Facebook page.

Your website is a place your customers can go and get the whole picture of who you are and what your business does.

Not all websites are good websites. And having a good website is important for most businesses. A good website is one that makes the business look professional and trustworthy.

Putting time, effort and money into your business website is important. For most businesses it should be considered as a high priority and one of the first online marketing tasks to be implemented.

Search Engine Optimisation

Search Engine Optimisation, or SEO, is the range of techniques used to get a website found on page one of a Google search.

It can take six months and even up to three years for the optimisation to get results, so SEO is a long-term strategy. It takes a lot of work to write content and to put techniques in place. Not only is it a long-term strategy, it is also a long-term commitment.

If being on page one of a Google search is not important for your business, don't worry about optimising your site.

Some examples of businesses that might prefer not to spend time and money on Search Engine Optimisation are businesses that:

- do a lot of face-to-face networking and generate leads this way
- find enough business through referrals, or
- intend to promote their business mainly on Facebook.

Having said that, a lot of businesses will benefit from being on page one of a Google search. If you feel this applies to you, start learning about Search Engine Optimisation.

Google Advertising

Like SEO, Google advertising will get a website found on page one of a Google search.

Unlike SEO, you need to pay Google directly for the privilege of being on page one. You don't need to wait six months or three years to get on page one of a Google search when you pay for Google advertising – you can get results the very next day.

If your business will benefit from being on page one of a Google search, and you can't wait for the longer-term benefits that optimising your site may bring, consider spending money on Google Advertising, also called Google Ads.

Social Media

We live in the Golden Age of Social Media. Many businesses have found they generate a lot of interest for their products or services on Facebook, Instagram, LinkedIn and other social media channels.

If you're a bakery, your Facebook page is likely to be doing really well. Handicrafts, hobbies, pet services, kids' classes, fashion and travel also do really well on Facebook.

The power of Facebook and LinkedIn as referral channels is outstanding. Tradies can, and do, pick up jobs as a result of a neighbour or friend tagging or recommending them on Facebook. The same applies with LinkedIn for various business-to-business service providers.

Having said that, many business owners over-estimate the power of social media to generate income for their business.

Many baby boomers in particular are not as savvy and quick to respond to potential customer queries as the channels demand. If you're not actively watching, responding and engaging with people on social media you could be losing potential customers to other businesses who are quicker off the mark.

You've got to be committed on these channels to really make an impact.

Facebook Advertising

If your customers are on Facebook and the products you sell, or services you provide, aren't boring, you may benefit from Facebook advertising.

You can also advertise on other social media channels such as LinkedIn, Instagram or YouTube.

If you struggle to keep up with the demand of constantly finding content and being creative with your posts, but you know Facebook is the right channel for your business, you may find paying Facebook, via Facebook advertising, a good strategy.

Email Marketing

Many business owners underestimate the power of email. Of all the digital marketing strategies it is one of the cheapest, easiest and most powerful to do – yet so many business owners shy away from it.

Email marketing is great for businesses that have longer-term, repeat or referral clients. It works exceptionally well with a strong networking strategy. Service industries where there's a high need for information, such as lawyers, accountants and business consultants, can benefit from a good email strategy.

Pick Your Battles

Pick the marketing activities that are strategically useful to your business. That may sound like an obvious statement, and it is, but many business owners procrastinate over their options and this often leads to either ad hoc or no marketing activity at all.

The Facebook Battle

One of the choices that confuse most business owners is around having a Facebook page. Most businesses should set up a business Facebook page. But what if you are an accountant? Most people are not hugely interested in being reminded about their tax returns when they are on Facebook!

There are three choices:

- have a business Facebook page and do a great job of it – hit it out of the ballpark
- have a business Facebook page and have it in 'housekeeping' mode, or
- don't have a business Facebook page.

Back to our accountant. My recommendation is this:

If the accountant, or their long-term staff member, loves Facebook and is super good at it, and can make tax fun on Facebook, then have a Facebook page for your accountancy business. Many times, business owners hit it out of the ballpark on a channel that isn't a natural fit for their industry, because they have the knack. Marketing is one of those things that if you genuinely love the platform, you're likely to be good at it. The key to this recommendation is '*you can make tax fun on Facebook.*' If you can't make it fun, maybe you shouldn't do it.

If you are an accountant and you don't really like Facebook, but you feel you must have a Facebook page, then do it in housekeeping mode. Don't over-service the channel. Post once a week, or once a fortnight, for the specific purpose of letting people know you are still in business. You're not doing it to generate new leads, your decision is around having a presence because you feel, or know, that some of your clients will need to see this as proof that you are open for business.

For most accountants their business will succeed without having a Facebook page. There's no need to procrastinate, worry, or be confused. It is what it is. Even though every other business appears to have a Facebook page, making you possibly think you should have one, if it doesn't generate leads or nurture prospects or help you grow and build your business, don't do it. It's that simple.

The Website Battle

Those three choices I mentioned pretty much exist for all the marketing options. Here's what it might look like for a website.

There are three choices:

- don't have one
- housekeeping mode, or
- hit it out of the ballpark.

In almost all cases I'd be recommending businesses have a website. I'm hard-pressed to think of one that shouldn't. Maybe if I was a petrol station owner I wouldn't have one as all of my business is generated by passing traffic. Signage, location and prices are the key marketing tools for a petrol station – a website is of little consequence.

A website in housekeeping mode is one that looks good, is informative and shows off your business to its best potential should someone visit it. And it's this last phrase that is the key – '*should someone visit it.*' A website in housekeeping mode isn't optimised for search engines, isn't having Google ads promoting it and the business owner doesn't have expectations that new leads will be generated. The website exists as a reference document, as an online brochure to back up the business sales team. It gives credibility to other marketing and sales activity.

If you know exactly who your customers are, for example if schools or real estate agents are your customers, the key lead-generation activity your business might consider is a phone campaign or knocking on doors or being present at trade shows. A website is important to have because you've directed people there and you want to look professional. Businesses like this could view their website as being in housekeeping mode.

But websites can do more than just exist and be present. They can be optimised to be found on page one of a Google search or they can have free giveaways in return for signing up for something. These tactics drive more people to your website and grow your business by doing everything possible to capture their contact details, so that you can continue a conversation with them beyond their first visit to your site. Many online businesses will benefit from a website that has lots of time and attention spent on it. And this is what I'd refer to as hitting it out of the ballpark. You're doing everything you can to make your website work for your business.

Housekeeping Mode

Housekeeping mode is a term I've coined for those marketing activities you feel you have to do but that are unlikely to generate new leads for your business in significant quantities. It may sound like an odd thing to encourage business owners to consider, but all too often I've come across business owners who procrastinate or waste hours and hours of time learning and implementing a marketing activity that is unlikely to generate compelling results.

Make a decision about the strategically important marketing activities for your business and differentiate them from the housekeeping marketing activities.

Marketing Plan

A lot of business owners try to do too much. It's just not possible to do everything. If you don't have a plan, if you don't have a strategy, you're likely to end up doing a lot of stuff badly. That's just a waste of time and rarely pays off.

Devote time and energy and commit to three strategically important marketing activities. Give the bare minimum of time and energy to the housekeeping marketing activities. And decide not to do some at all – your time and resources are too precious to waste.

It's highly likely at least one of the three strategically important marketing activities will be digital. There are so many potential customers researching products and services online, it is unlikely your business will succeed if it is not robustly working at least one online channel.

It's highly likely at least one of your marketing activities will not be a digital one. For most small businesses, face-to-face networking, referrals, trade shows or personal contact of some kind remains an important marketing activity.

Three activities gives you enough that if one doesn't work, you still have another two that will grow your business. More than three and you are spreading yourself too thin and unlikely to be doing a good job of any of them.

Most strategically important marketing activities will require at least six months, and some a year, before you can determine if they are working. Many business owners give up after three weeks or give a marketing activity minimal effort. But most marketing requires time and committed effort to work. Quite a lot of digital marketing requires trial and error to implement. Channels like Google and Facebook have complicated algorithms that need analysing and then optimising. Think of it as artificial intelligence – these systems require time and experience with your brand, keywords and audience choices, to find the sweet spot for your advertising.

Impact, Confidence and Ease (ICE)

Clo Willaerts in her book *"Digital Marketing Like a PRO: Prepare. Run. Optimize."* introduces the ICE score as a framework for making a decision about what digital marketing activity to do. ICE stands for **I**mpact, **C**onfidence and **E**ase. What marketing activities do you think will have the best impact for your business? What marketing activities are you confident will work and you can implement? Will there be hurdles for you to overcome that will delay the roll-out? How easy will you find it to do the marketing? By thinking about these questions, and giving them a score out of 10, the ICE framework will give your marketing plan direction.

I've slightly adjusted her framework, to include both digital and non-digital channels, to help you prioritise your three key marketing activities. The three marketing activities that you will hit it out of the ballpark with. The ones you are going to commit time, money and resources to.

On the next page there is an example of an ICE table that lists all the possible marketing strategies a business could think of. Each strategy has been given a score for Impact & Effectiveness and Confidence & Ease.

Strategy	**Impact & Effectiveness** (out of 10)	**Confidence & Ease** (out of 10)	**Score** (out of 20: add up previous two columns)	**Priority** (pick the top three scores)
Website	7	4	11	
Email Marketing	7	5	12	3
Facebook	3	8	11	
LinkedIn	7	9	16	1
SEO	4	5	9	
Google Ads	6	3	9	
Networking	9	6	15	2
Phone calls	7	2	9	
Trade shows	4	7	11	
TV advertising	8	0	8	
Radio advertising	8	3	11	
PR/media campaign	9	2	11	

In the example above the marketing plan would focus on LinkedIn, Networking and Email Marketing, as these have the highest scores. Draw up your own list and see what three marketing activities come up best for your business.

Implementation

A lot of marketing fails due to bad implementation.

Most failures are due to inaction or a lazy approach. Sometimes this is driven by an anti-marketing attitude. Many start-up small businesses feel that if the product they have or the service they offer is great, they will naturally succeed. This is rarely the case. You may not like marketing and you may like digital marketing even less, but without a plan to reach out to potential customers and win them over to become buyers, your business is likely to fail.

Many business owners see marketing, and in particular, online marketing as 'the dark arts'. They don't know how to get started or they make an attempt and get confused with all the jargon and language.

My hope for this book is that it gives you guidance and motivation to start, or re-energise, your digital marketing efforts.

Next Steps – What you can do

List all the possible marketing strategies that could apply to your business. Score each one out of 10 for:

- » the impact you expect it will have to generate leads
- » your own confidence level and expectation of how easy it will be for you to do (either by doing it yourself or hiring a specialist)

Add those two scores together. Pick the three strategies with the top scores. Commit to these strategies for at least six, preferably 12, months.

If you end up with a mix that just doesn't feel right – maybe they are all digital channels with no face-to-face opportunities – or vice-versa – they are all personal networking options and no digital – then re-jig the plan to what feels right.

For some business owners, you may need to deliberately undertake an activity you don't like and that you are not naturally good at. If marketing doesn't come easily for you, you may need to spend time practicing and learning or seeking the help of a mentor, coach or trainer.

Write down your plan and goals

- » write down your yearly goal for each strategy
- » write down three monthly goals for each strategy
- » write down activities that will help you reach the goals (perhaps a weekly or fortnightly task)

- put the goals, activities and tasks in your calendar, to-do list, project management software or wherever/whatever you use to keep your business activities on track

Rinse and repeat

As you achieve your goals, set new ones.

If you don't achieve them in the time allocated, repeat them for the next time period – perhaps setting a lower or higher expectation for yourself, depending on circumstances. If you've changed your mind about a goal – perhaps it isn't likely to have the impact you expected, or you find that it's way out of your comfort level – let it go. Move on.

Every three months, revise your goals and satisfy yourself that they remain worthy of being on your radar.

The butterfly test

Set your goals high enough that they give you butterflies in your tummy (i.e. a sign you're being challenged). But not so high that they cause anxiety. A little challenge is good, but nobody needs an overdose of stress!

TEMPLATE
Goal Planning

My One Year Goal is:

Goal for 1st Quarter:

Fortnightly tasks that will help me reach this goal:

☐ Yes, this goal will help me reach my one year goal

Goal for 2nd Quarter:

Fortnightly tasks that will help me reach this goal:

☐ Yes, this goal will help me reach my one year goal

Goal for 3rd Quarter:

Fortnightly tasks that will help me reach this goal:

☐ Yes, this goal will help me reach my one year goal

Goal for 4th Quarter:

Fortnightly tasks that will help me reach this goal:

☐ Yes, this goal will help me reach my one year goal

☐ Yes, I've added tasks into my business planner

TEMPLATE
Marketing Strategy

Strategy	**Impact & Effectiveness** (out of 10)	**Confidence & Ease** (out of 10)	**Score** (out of 20: add up previous two columns)
Website			
SEO			
Google Advertising			
Email Marketing			
Email Sales Funnel			
Facebook			
Facebook Ads			
LinkedIn			
Instagram			
Twitter			
YouTube			
eBay			
Airbnb			
Gumtree			
hipages			
Networking			
Trade Shows			
Markets			
Phone Campaigns			
TV Advertising			
Radio Advertising			
PR/Media			
Other:			
Other:			

My Top 3 Marketing Strategies Are:

1.

2.

3.

Case Study: Jeweller — Choosing Top 3 Marketing Activities

Amy, a silver jeweller, specialises in creating beautiful pendants of Australian animals and outback icons. She has spent the last two years selling her jewellery at markets and online through her website. But sales are low and she's had to re-think her marketing and sales strategy. Amy listed all the marketing and sales channels she could think of in the first column of the marketing decision table.

She gave each one a score out of ten for how comfortable she felt with it, and a score out of ten for how effective she thought each strategy would be. Although she likes doing markets (they scored a 10 in that column), she rated their effectiveness at making sales a low three, giving markets an overall score of 13.

The top three marketing strategies as identified in Amy's template were:

- Tourist gift shops
- Etsy
- SEO

Tourist gift shops

Given the pendants feature Australian animals and outback icons, Amy is convinced if she can get more tourist gift shops to stock her jewellery, her business will thrive. She already has one gift shop that is a slow, but steady, sales channel for her. The process of listing all the possibilities and then rating them identified for Amy that even though she feels some anxiety about approaching gift shops (she scored her ease a low four), she felt the long-term success of this strategy was high and scored it 10. She has now set herself a goal of approaching three tourist gift shops a month over the next 12 months. Her aim is to get into 10 shops.

Etsy

Etsy is an e-commerce platform that specialises in bespoke and handcrafted items and Amy's jewellery is a good fit. A friend and creative colleague of hers sells her wooden homewares on this channel and has had a lot of success. Because Amy has decided on Etsy as being in her top three, not only will she list the jewellery items on Etsy, she will learn how to optimise her items to ensure they get good results in the Etsy listings when people search for Australian jewellery. She's even prepared to spend some money on promoting the listings for even better exposure.

SEO

Although her current online sales are low, Amy has heard about Search Engine Optimisation, and feels that if she's learning techniques on how to optimise her Etsy listings, there will be some cross-over learning with how to optimise her website for Google searches. Having been to a recent workshop on SEO, she feels confident she can do this (she gave it a score of 8). She also gave it an impact score of 8, giving SEO an overall score of 16.

Markets

Amy's most comfortable channel was markets, which had a score of 13. This was just behind tourist gift shops (14), Etsy (15) and SEO (16). As she loves doing markets and they create an opportunity for her to talk to people about her jewellery and get feedback and ideas, she's decided to retain the big market prior to Christmas held at a popular tourist destination a few hours drive from her, but stop doing the other smaller ones that haven't returned many sales.

With these decisions now made, Amy feels confident that she knows exactly where to focus her energies for the next 12 months for business success.

Case Study: Business Coach — Choosing Top 3 Marketing Activities

Adam is a business consultant providing coaching to CEOs and middle managers. His main business is providing face-to-face coaching and mentoring, however he has recently branched out to provide coaching via video conference calls, to expats living in Asia.

The top three marketing strategies Adam's list identified were:

» Networking

» LinkedIn

» PR/Media

Networking

Networking has always worked for Adam, and he enjoys it. It scored a high 19. Now with a more determined outlook, he plans to focus his networking on bigger events and conferences with inspirational keynote speakers that attract leaders from large corporations. By focusing his networking efforts on specific events and occasions, he feels he will meet more of the people that are likely to be interested in his services.

LinkedIn

Like networking, LinkedIn has been a good channel for Adam. He keeps an active profile with updates 2-3 times a week. The process of planning his marketing has re-energised him and he has committed to writing and publishing an article once a month on LinkedIn, which he has heard works well to boost your profile. In particular he'll use this channel to discuss Australian-Asian business challenges and opportunities, which he hopes will attract some of the expats to his coaching business.

What surprised Adam from the results of this exercise was his decision to stop his Twitter channel and Facebook page. They take up a lot of time, and he's identified that these social media channels aren't really effective for him.

PR/Media

Another surprise for Adam was the inclusion of the PR/Media strategy. He has not actively pursued media opportunities for his business, but upon scoring it he realised he would love to do this (in his younger days he was a journalist for a small country paper) and he feels it would have a good impact in attracting the right kind of clients.

Case Study: Cake Shop — Goal Setting

Sally runs a small cake making business. Up until now, she has used Facebook and Instagram as her main marketing channels. Both Facebook and Instagram have worked well for her and she credits them with giving her the success she's had so far.

Two years ago, when she first started out, a friend developed a website for her. It's already looking out of date and it's never portrayed the warmth and fun-loving spirit she likes to bring into her business and cake making.

Although she remains committed to using social media to market her business, the website is where she can send people to get a good overall picture of her business. To that end she has committed to improving it and set herself a 3 month goal to get good quality pictures of herself, her business and the cakes for the website.

To assist with this goal, she's set herself fortnightly tasks that she's written down in her business calendar.

Fortnight 1: research and book professional photographer for head shot.

Fortnight 2: learn how to download cake photos from phone and file on computer for use on website.

Fortnight 3: ask cousin Denise, family photography enthusiast, to take some outside photos of the shop.

Fortnight 4: purchase white fabric or board and set up a corner in the shop to take professional cake photos. The white background and good natural lighting will enhance the look of future cake photos.

Fortnight 5: using the new photo corner, take photos of the cakes as they are made, and before delivery to the customer.

Reference

Digital Marketing like a Pro; Prepare. Run. Optimise, by Clo Willaerts. Lannoo Campus Publishers, Belgium. 2018.

CHAPTER 2

DO-IT-YOURSELF VS PAY A PROFESSIONAL

Do-It-Yourself

A lot of sole traders and small businesses try not to hire people to do marketing for their business or to build their website. Sometimes this do-it-yourself activity is driven by necessity – you may be starting the business on an absolute shoe-string budget and you're unable to find those extra dollars to fund marketing expenses. Some of it, however, is driven by the many do-it-yourself online tools, and the advertising accompanying these tools, that promote how easy they are to use.

Well, of course, if you've built an online platform that can build a website, generate leads, or design a logo, you're going to promote how easy it is to use. The sad reality for those of us who are baby boomers is that while some of us might find it easy, many of us won't.

And even for those, of any age, who find it easy, will the product they get be any good? It's fine to have online tools that help you develop a logo, but are your visual discretionary powers able to ascertain if it's any good? If you want a memorable, standout logo then paying a professional graphic designer to do the job is the best choice. If having an average logo is sufficient for your business, then doing it yourself might be a good option.

Starting any business will involve some investment. Doing it yourself may save you money in the short-term but you may find you spend lots of time and money not getting the results you need. Many digital marketing activities, like online advertising and websites, benefit from having people with experience leading the project.

Many clients I talk to only want to learn what they need to know. But they don't know what they don't know. Often they miss out on important information because they are not aware of the possibilities. Experienced professionals know the possibilities and keep up with the latest features.

I love the resourcefulness and independence of business owners. I thrive on helping business owners learn how to do stuff themselves. But some don't quite find the right balance. They overestimate their abilities and underestimate the number of traps and tricks that exist with the online platforms.

Computer Literacy

Many baby boomer business owners struggle with computer literacy. Computers are difficult. Learning doesn't happen overnight. It happens with a committed effort.

If you are running a business, you need to have basic computer literacy. You may not be aware that you don't know the basics. If things frequently upset you when you're using the computer, it's likely you have low computer literacy.

I urge you to consider taking a computer course and learning the basics if you struggle in this area. Basic computer literacy would include knowing the following:

- what a browser is
- how to refresh a browser
- how to take a screenshot
- how to file an electronic document
- how to rename a computer file
- how to download a photo from your phone to your computer

If you don't understand the above list, or you are not confident about being able to do some of these things, it's very likely that you would benefit from taking a computer course or one-on-one computer training.

In Australia, libraries have been proactive in helping people learn computer skills. If you think you could benefit from one-on-one computer help, contact your local library. Or find a computer course near you. If you prefer one-on-one help, in most capital cities, there are private operators who offer one-on-one training.

Many baby boomers know how to use a computer but they've missed out on the theory. Going to a course will give you that theory and help you learn how to troubleshoot when things go wrong.

If you don't know the basics, you're not a good candidate for creating your own website or managing your own online marketing.

Paying a Professional

A local provider could and should (in my opinion) interpret and help explain things along the way. They can guide you in making an informed decision. They should be translating the jargon (or not using it) so you understand the decisions you are making and how your money is being spent.

For some baby boomer business people, it's not the jargon that concerns them, it's distrust in the strategy. Marketing is a bit fluffy and online advertising is almost akin to the dark arts. There are some hard statistics backing up many marketing practices, but not all. Some marketing decisions are still based on gut feeling and a willingness to take a risk. If you're unsure about whether the strategy will be successful or not, ask your service provider to give you a realistic assessment of what to expect from your expenditure. Ask them how many other businesses, like yours, they have done this for and what results did they get.

Added to the jargon and lack of trust is the bad experience that quite a few business owners have had with website developers and marketing agencies. There are more than a few sharks in the industry! While providers should interpret the jargon, it's still important for business owners to make an effort to learn the lingo and be realistic about what to expect from marketing activities. Learn enough so you can understand the conversation with your specialists and the consequences of your decisions. Don't agree to part with your money unless you understand what services are being provided to you.

Next Steps – What you can do

Be realistic about where your strengths are. All businesses require some investment and incur costs. Are you better off doing it yourself or hiring someone?

Learn and keep learning. The fact that you're reading this means you appreciate you've got some learning to do. Good on you – keep at it!

Websites: Do-It-Yourself or Pay a Developer

Do-It-Yourself Website

Websites can, and do, present businesses in an unprofessional light if they look like an amateur built them. Do-it-yourself business owners may find their website has technical errors because they don't have the same experience as the professionals. Websites need to be aesthetically pleasing and technically solid – often neither of these things are commented on when they are correct – but they're certainly noticed when they're wrong!

Building your own website is not as easy as some of the adverts make it sound.

Platforms like Wix, Weebly and Squarespace are easier than WordPress. Shopify is supposedly easy, but as soon as you want to do something a little interesting with the platform, it becomes difficult. They are all harder than Facebook.

If you've never edited a website before, you're likely to find developing one from scratch a very steep learning curve. Think of it like building a house. If you've never used a hammer, renovated a kitchen, knocked down a wall, built a pergola or any one of the other numerous house renovation tasks that are possible, how would you go building a house from scratch? You might be able to build a house without the renovator's experience, but knowing a few tricks of the trade before you embarked on such a big project would certainly give you a head start.

There are lots of different platforms available to create a website. Many make it sound easy to use their software and create a fantastic looking site. It is possible to make a website yourself, but very few of us would call it easy. It's even harder to make a site that looks good, attracts and converts visitors to customers, and is technically solid.

Don't get caught out that they're free. The free options come with tacky branding or tacky adverts (or both).

Be aware that some of the platforms have add-ons that cost money. The original offer could have a tempting monthly or annual cost, but you may end up paying more in the second and subsequent years as the first year was a sweetener deal. Or, as you go through the process, you realise a needed bit of functionality or usefulness was not included in the original payment. This is where the experience and knowledge of a professional website developer counts.

You can you build your own website. The fact is that tools are out there now that weren't available five or ten years ago. But don't underestimate the computer knowledge required.

For those who have good computer skills, the other consideration is your design capability. Many do-it-yourself business owners end up creating a site that looks tacky or clunky. If you're intent on building your own site, and design isn't your key skill, keep it simple.

If you are building your own site, the best option is to develop it using the easier, all-in-one fully hosted builders. Popular all-in-one builders are Wix, Weebly and Squarespace. It's much easier to build and edit a website using these proprietary branded platforms, than it is using WordPress (for example), as most of the technical stuff is taken care of.

Your website is the window into your business – customers are looking in and checking up on you – are you happy with what they see? It's important your website looks professional and speaks to your customers. Although I admire the resourcefulness of the do-it-yourself business owner, I rarely admire the website they've developed for themselves.

Local Website Developer

If you go down the path of paying a developer, look at their portfolio – what other websites have they made? Do you like them? If you like the other websites they've developed, you're likely to like the website they make for you. If they don't have an online portfolio, ask them to send you the links to websites they've developed in the last 12 months.

Most website builds typically require a lot of back-and-forth communication. As a client, you'll probably have questions around the design options or have comments you'd like to feed into the process. Being able to pick up the phone or meet your website developer in person helps make the process, and usually the website itself, a success.

Once the website is built, think about how they will hand over the keys to you. What training will they provide? Unfortunately many developers overstate the training they'll give and underestimate how hard it will be for you. Like the adverts, they say it'll be easy. That means it's easy for them. It doesn't mean it's easy for you.

Most professional website developers use the self-managed WordPress.org. In fact it's the most popular website builder, with over 30% of the world's websites using it. WordPress is more flexible than the all-in-one platforms and gives developers the opportunity to build a site that is specific to your requirements.

To add to the confusion there are two WordPress platforms, not unlike the Catholics and Protestants. Both Christians, but there was a parting of ways somewhere in the past. Stumbling across the less popular all-in-one WordPress.com option is a common mistake.

WordPress.org websites need to be maintained. The software needs updating. This is done for you with the all-in-one platforms, but not so with WordPress.org. As well as asking your developer about training, be sure to talk with them about the responsibility and cost for keeping the site's software up-to-date.

With a local website developer you'll be able to draw upon their experience and knowledge of what looks good and works online. You'll have a sounding board for your business ideas and how they translate to the online environment.

I'm biased of course, because I own and manage a website development agency, but I'd recommend a local developer for your website build above doing it yourself or any of the other options.

Freelancers

Some business owners may use Fiverr, Freelancer or another online platform to find their website developer. If you know exactly what you are looking for, using an online freelancer could work for you. However, most businesses owners aren't sure what they need. Here are some questions to help you understand if you know what you are looking for:

- Do you need a Wix, Shopify, WordPress or custom-built site? Do you know enough about these platforms to know which one is best for you?
- Do you know how to write up the specifications for your website so they are clear and unambiguous for the freelancer you are hiring?
- Do you know exactly what you want for the text and images on the site?
- What training or hand-over plan is there for your site once the freelancer has finished his or her job?

If you have a clear understanding about what you want and how to manage the process during and after the build, an online freelancer could be a good choice for you. However, if you have little knowledge about what you are asking for, you're likely to end up getting what you don't want or need.

A local developer is likely to be easier to communicate with than an online freelancer. Website builds typically require a lot of communication, as there are usually lots of questions and lots of decisions. These questions can be asked and answered by email, but often a real-time voice, or face-to-face conversation makes it easier to trouble-shoot the more complex decisions.

A trend in recent years is for local website businesses in Australia (and possibly US, Canada and UK) to hire online freelancers, often in a different country, to build the site for their customers, often without the customer's knowledge. These sites are typically built in WordPress, have highly coded front pages and over-complicated themes. They usually come with no training on hand-over. In their defence, they usually look great. However, as a result of the high level of coding and the theme used, the customer, and the agency they hired, are often unable to edit or update the site at a later stage. We've seen many upset clients to whom this has happened.

Often a phone call, where you can speak directly to the website developer, can greatly assist in moving a website project along in the right direction. Email is great as a communication tool, but sometimes the nuances get missed. I don't mind working in our global world and hiring talented people from various parts of the globe, but a website is a multi-layered project. Outsourcing the development of it is fraught with difficulties.

We've found hiring people overseas, where the communication is only by email, to be good on smaller tasks that are very specific. For example, we sometimes look for specific IT expertise from a highly specialised person and they just happen to live somewhere different from us. In this case hiring an overseas freelancer makes sense. I'm not convinced it makes sense for a website build.

Next Steps – What you can do

Decide on the best website platform for you – don't leave it to chance or let someone else decide for you. It is a major decision and impacts on what can and can't be done. Research the reasons for and against the various platforms.

If you're hiring a website developer, ask them lots of questions. Hire them if you feel confident they are the right fit for you. It's a long-term relationship as you're likely to be in contact with them in 6 months, a year and 2 years when the site needs an update or something goes wrong.

If you're doing it yourself, expect many late nights watching YouTube video tutorials and reading online help articles. Leave plenty of time, don't work to a tight deadline – keep your stress levels in check.

Case Study: Marketing Business — WordPress Website Development

In 2017, Amelia, who owned a marketing business, chose to have her website developed by a freelancer found on the job posting site Upwork. This was a cheaper option than using a local developer.

She had some experience with WordPress but not so much that she wanted to build her own site. She found a WordPress template she liked and this was used for the build.

There were significant communication difficulties and Amelia described the process as a nightmare. She found herself tearing her hair out several times (figuratively speaking).

It took much longer to build the site than she expected.

Although she didn't know it at the time, the look of her site was created with specialised coding, over and above what the template provided. This made it difficult to update the site, and years later she is struggling to keep the site up-to-date as the coding conflicts with newer versions of some of the software.

Part of the problem stemmed from the inability to discuss the pros and cons of going ahead with certain requests or ideas. Amelia felt like she was making decisions in a knowledge vacuum.

She's very happy with the look of the site but is not happy that updates and edits are difficult to make.

In addition, there was no training on hand-over, so she had to stumble along in the dark trying to figure things out.

Case Study: Finance Business — WordPress Website Development

Unfortunately, even using a local developer does not always guarantee good service, as a small, boutique finance business found out the hard way.

This business already had a website but wanted a more professional one they could update themselves. They wanted to be able to keep the information on their site relevant and fresh.

The site lacked warmth and looked generic. It looked like any other finance business, significantly because stock images were used. The site wasn't personal to them and their business, even though they met with the developer 3 or 4 times.

The co-owner of this business, Caroline, is very computer literate. She uses computers every day, has software unique to the finance industry which she regularly uses and has advanced skills in Excel.

Even so, during the process Caroline felt there was a lot of jargon used and the website developer blinded them with technology.

On handover they were given a piece of paper with instructions on how to change and update the text. She didn't have previous experience in editing websites, the instructions weren't helpful and there was no support or ongoing help to assist them update it. Even though they were paying a monthly fee, they didn't know what this covered but evidently it didn't cover help or training

> to edit the site. This is in stark contrast to the finance software they use that provides a good support help desk.
>
> It seems to them that the web company built the site and then washed their hands of it.
>
> The site ended up not getting updated for a few years and when the final update was made, major errors occurred which then needed fixing.
>
> As a business, the finance company provides ongoing care and support to their customers. They expect this from their suppliers. They would have been happy to pay for ongoing site support, but it just wasn't there for them, even at a price.

Search Engine Optimisation (SEO): Do-It-Yourself or Pay a Specialist

Many businesses have had bad experiences with, or don't trust, SEO specialists.

This comes about because:

- it's technically a hard area and this makes it difficult to explain to clients
- there are many highly focused IT specialists who don't have communication as one of their better skills
- business owners don't question the specialists enough or learn to understand the lingo
- the techniques are ever-changing so both specialist and client find it hard to keep up

- there are a few bad apples, i.e. SEO specialists who are ripping clients off

Many business owners have given up on Search Engine Optimisation, or never started, or have been burnt. There are certainly many who can't afford the extraordinary fees being charged.

So what to do?

If you're a business owner, decide first whether SEO is important to you. If it is and you are hiring someone to do it for you, ask to see screen shots of their work – examples of links they have secured for you or Google webpage summaries (i.e. meta-descriptions) they have written. Learn to read the report, what it means and what the key performance indicators are for your business.

The CEO of a business is expected to, and should be able to, read the profit and loss statement the accountant prepares and understand terms such as current assets vs fixed assets. If you're responsible for running the business, you're responsible for understanding the reports presented to you by specialist staff. You need to be able to read, interpret and make decisions about what your SEO person does. If you can't read the report, learn to.

Better yet, work in partnership with your SEO person. Ask them what you can do to support the work they are doing. Chances are, there is stuff you can write that will assist their work. You know your business better than anyone else and you are the best person to write about your services and products.

If you are intending to do-it-yourself read the chapter in this book that gives you ideas and know-how. The good news is that doing some Search Engine Optimisation is better than doing none, and even some is likely to generate good results for businesses in a low to medium competitive environment. It's generally not wasted time.

Learning SEO takes time, practice and understanding the jargon.

Next Steps – What you can do

Decide if you need to optimise your website for Search Engines.

If you do, read the chapter on SEO in this book.

If you don't – don't do it.

Online Ads: Do-It-Yourself or Pay a Consultant

Business owners can certainly learn how to do their own online advertising, but there are traps for inexperienced players with both Google and Facebook.

Consultants and agencies who specialise in this area often over-service. What I mean by this is that if you are a dog groomer and all you need is a basic click to website advert, you might get talked into re-marketing ads or other advanced campaigns. While those advanced campaigns are great and do work a treat, for very small businesses they are often too much. If you can get enough new clients through the door with a basic advert, why pay a high monthly administration cost to get a more advanced advert you don't need?

But even the basic adverts are difficult to set up and both platforms have methods for extracting more money from you than necessary. Both platforms make it easy to create under-performing ads and make it hard to create ads that work. Funny how the tick boxes often default to the unnecessary and expensive options!

The beauty with online advertising is that you can test with a relatively small amount of money and see the results the next day. Understanding and optimising the adverts based on those results and reports takes experience and learning.

Next Steps – What you can do

If Google Ads or Facebook advertising is one of your three strategically important marketing activities, be sure to read the chapter in this book. Take a course in online advertising – discover all you can about how it works.

CHAPTER 3

CUSTOMER PROFILE

Why Have a Customer Profile

A customer profile is something that puzzles a lot of small business owners.

A customer profile is a pretend person who you've written down and described – the profile of a person most like your ideal customer. The one who spends most money with you, comes back time and again to make more purchases and is likely to talk about your business to their friends.

The customer profile is a tool to assist you in writing content and making choices about who to market your business to.

The profile includes their name, age, how they spend their time, where they live and who makes up their family and household. It includes what events they like to go to, what books they like to read or their favourite movies, quotes or heroes. As it is a pretend person, you make this up from your imagination, based on who you know to be, or think would be, the person with the most interest in the products you sell or the services you provide.

In response to being asked to describe their ideal customer, a lot of small business owners will say 'everyone'. To a certain extent that is true. If you own a shop and someone walks in and they want to buy something, you'd sell it to them. So, in that sense, everyone is your customer.

But a customer profile is not describing who you'll sell to, it's describing who you'll market to.

It's about where you're going to spend your resources, your time and your money to promote your product or service. Who are you going to target?

It's cheaper to target a few people than it is a large group. For that reason, knowing exactly who you're promoting your business to is a very good idea. Done right, it should help you decide upon your three key marketing activities.

Beyond that, it's a useful tool to help you write content for a Facebook post, your website pages or your next blog article. What you're going to write about and the tone of voice you use is determined by who you're writing for.

For example, if your ideal customer is a senior public servant who makes the purchasing decisions for a government department, you'd use words and phrases based around that person. However, if your ideal customer is a young adult looking to make an impact on the world, you'd speak in a different tone and choose different online platforms to have a presence on.

You may have heard marketing people talk about a customer avatar. This is the same as a customer profile. Whether we call it a 'customer profile' or a 'customer avatar' doesn't really matter – we're talking about the same thing – we're talking about building a picture of who your ideal customer is.

The ideal customer is the one that will spend the most money with you; the customer that will keep coming back to get more of your services or products; the customer that will talk about you to their friends and be your ambassador. That's your ideal customer. So, think about your ideal customer, the one who's going to love what you do or what you sell and that's the one we want to build this profile around.

Let's think about another tool we use in our lives. Let's say we've just bought an orange tree from the garden shop and we're going to dig a hole in the garden to put the plant in. The spade you use to do this is a tool. It's just a tool to help you get a job done. It's much easier than using your hands and you'll dig a much bigger hole with a spade than you would with just your bare hands.

So, the customer profile is the spade. It's a tool. You're going to use your customer profile as a tool to help you market and promote your business. It's not going to stop you selling to people who don't fit the exact profile. It doesn't define your whole business or change the way you view customers who don't fit the profile. It's going to assist you in making the right offers to the right people at the right time and in the right places.

It's going to help you to write your next LinkedIn update or blog article. It's going to help you choose the right audiences if you advertise on Facebook or Google.

How to Create a Customer Profile

Now that we've accepted that a customer profile is a useful tool, we'll talk about how we create it.

Give your customer profile a name typical of their era. For example, if your ideal customer is born in the 1990s you might name them Jessica or Ben. But if your ideal customer was born in the 1940s you might name them Thelma or Stan. Names are a bit fashionable, aren't they? So, pick a name that is typical of the era of your customer.

One of my customer profiles is called 'Determined Denise'. I've given her an additional adjective to help describe her, which you can do too.

Start adding in more details like:

- where they live (country, region, province, state, city or suburb)
- what sort of income or disposable income they have
- education
- what books they like to read
- what events they like to go to

What we're doing here is bringing this pretend person to life. Giving them a persona that we can relate to. This helps get them into our head.

Pain Points

Next, we want to talk about what their challenges and their pain points are in relation to what you sell. If they hate flying, that might be a challenge for them, but unless you're selling plane tickets we don't really care about that. What we care about is what their pain point is, or what their challenge is, as it relates to your product or service.

Let's say you sell water pumps and someone within proximity of your business has just bought a hobby farm. They've gone from working as an experienced corporate financier to an inexperienced hobby farmer.

Their farm has a dam and, for the first time in this person's life, they need to buy a water pump. What are the pain points and challenges for them in buying a water pump? Now, this is important as you've probably forgotten what it's like to buy a water pump for the first time. The nerves you had about buying your first water pump are long gone.

As a seller of water pumps, you know all about them. Many of the typical questions that customers ask you about water pumps is what this tree-changing ex-corporate financier is wanting to know.

Tree-change hobby farmers are your ideal customers – so you want to keep reminding yourself of what it's like to be in their shoes.

Write your customer profile so that it includes the pain points (anxieties, nervousness or challenges) as they relate to your ideal customer, who's making this purchase for the first time. For our new hobby farmer it might be that he feels out of control and lacks knowledge. In his previous job he was a leader in his field, now he's swapped that life for stuff he doesn't know a lot about.

Use the profile to give you direction on what online platforms to seek out to promote your product. There are bound to be agricultural websites or social media pages which hobby farmers turn to for advice. By thinking about your customer, your presence on these sites will not only be about the pump specifications, it will also include what applications, areas or situations the pump is best suited to. Your customer profile might inspire you to include local references, not just the stock standard product description coming from the manufacturer. Make your online presence personal, connected and relevant to your customer profile.

Another trick to help in this process is to go back to your first week in business or the first time you became involved in what it is you're selling. This will bring back memories about what the pain points are for your first-time customers.

First-Time Purchase

Your first-time customer is quite important in marketing. We know that in running a business, having repeat customers is the best thing to get. It will cost a lot less in time and money to make a sale to somebody who's already bought from you than somebody new. So that's really good. There are a lot of things you can do in digital marketing to nurture customers to keep them coming back. Good old-fashioned customer service and great products are, of course, essential to this. However in developing a customer profile, we want to concentrate on the person who's never heard of you.

Sometimes it can work well to think about the apprentice, or the person who is doing work experience. These people work for your established clients and customers, but they are new to the job. They need more information and explanation than the more experienced staff members.

What activities can you do online, and in the digital space, to get people who don't know you exist, into your business?

Let's imagine that new employee Hannah has been given the job of buying 20 metres of electrical roofing cable for an urgent job that has been scheduled in for tomorrow. She might start with the previous invoices from cable suppliers or she might just Google '*electric cable for roofing in office buildings*'.

Will she find your online shop? If you've put words in your description that connect with the kinds of things she's searching for, there's more chance she'll find your online shop. She's not using words like conduit, poly, earth, stranded, core and other specification values, she's using the words cable, roofing and office. I'm by no means suggesting you don't have good quality information for your product descriptions – please keep including specification values. But add to that more information about when and where the product gets used. Thinking about the new employee, apprentice, trainee or work experience person, and what they might search on to find your products, could help inspire your writing.

You want to inform and educate your first-time customer in a way that they understand, addresses their pain points and gives them confidence that your business is the right place to help them.

Objections to Sale

You may wish to include in your customer avatar what their objection to sale commonly is. Common objections to sale are:

- not enough money
- don't trust the business
- don't know enough about the business
- haven't researched other options

Thinking about the objections to sale for this person will remind you of what you need to consider when writing product brochures, submitting quotes or speaking with clients over the phone.

Use your customer profile to help you write good content. Content is great for website visitors and great for Search Engine Optimisation. Use the profile to give you inspiration, to target your message effectively and to write product and service descriptions authentically and convincingly.

Don't try to be everything to everyone because you'll end up being nothing to no one. Try and be something to someone, and that someone is your customer profile.

Next Steps – What you can do

Get stuck into writing, or updating, your Customer Profile.

Give them a name. Understand what their challenges or anxieties might be around purchasing your services. Bring them to life with details like their age, where they live and what books they like to read or activities they enjoy.

Print it out.

Laminate it.

Keep the profile somewhere handy in your office and bring it out when you're writing your next blog article, product description or Facebook post.

Case Study: Bookkeeper – Customer Profile

Project Pete

Owner of a business which has a niche, good quality product.

Age: 35

Partnership status: In a relationship

Children: A two-year old

Location: Seaside suburb in capital city

Job: Solopreneur

Annual Income: $40,000 + investment property

Level of Education: Secondary School

Hobby: Plays football

Pete's goal

To unleash his product onto the world

Pete values

Efficiency and effectiveness

Pete's favourite quote

'As an entrepreneur, one of the biggest challenges you will face will be building your brand. The ultimate goal is to set your company and your brand apart from the crowd.'
Ryan Holmes

Challenges

Not enough time

Pain Points

Cashflow

Objections to Sale

Are you as good as I am – how do I know?

Admitting the need to have someone else on his team – giving up control

Role in the Purchase Decision

Sole decision maker

TEMPLATE
Customer Profile

Name

Age

Partnership status

Children

Location

Job

Annual Income

Level of Education

Hobby

Goal

Values

Favourite quote

Challenges

Pain Points

Objections to Sale

Role in the Purchase Decision

CHAPTER 4

WHEN IT ALL GOES WRONG

Most baby boomers find it frustrating when something goes wrong with a computer or the device we're using. It's understandable – technology is changing at an ever-increasing rate – and many of us are struggling to keep up.

Online marketing, by its very nature, uses these ever-changing online tools and platforms. Using the technology is unavoidable for today's business.

Usernames, Passwords and Login Details

Online tools and platforms require accounts and login details. Not knowing the usernames and passwords to online accounts is the most common thing that prevents business owners from being able to use online platforms.

One of the reasons business owners don't know their login details is because they use the 'remember me' function on login. This tends to result in people forgetting their usernames and passwords as they're not regularly needing to use them. It's great the computer can remember it, but as soon as you work on another computer, change location or need to give your username to an IT person, you're often unable to.

Google and other platforms often require a secondary verification step where they send a text to a mobile phone number. This can also upset the applecart. The number they'll insist on sending it to is the one recorded in their system. If you're using someone else's Google account – your boss's, partner's or workmate's – this often prevents you from being able to log in – especially if you're at a training event or at a different location than usual.

It is your responsibility to know and be able to access details for software, sites and platforms you have accounts with. If you are unsure of your login details, this indicates you don't have a system for recording and retrieving your usernames and passwords.

I recommended you create a system that works for you. Without one, the process of online marketing, especially when you're working with others, becomes frustrating.

Try keeping your passwords written down in an unlikely-looking book kept in a safe place, or use an app that remembers passwords, or a spreadsheet to keep track of your logins. Your memory is unlikely to be a good method and has proven to be unreliable for most of us.

Technical Issues

If you're struggling with a technical issue, the following will help your IT person to help you:

- a clear description of what is going wrong
- the device (e.g. mobile phone model, desktop computer make and model)
- the browser (e.g. Chrome, Firefox, Safari)

- the name of the software, site or platform being used when the issue happened
- the name of the buttons, links, fields or areas on the site you were clicking on leading up to the issue
- the web address or URL where the problem happens
- the error message wording
- a screenshot

If you haven't yet worked out how to take a screenshot, here are a few tips:

PC: use Print Screen from the keyboard
PC: use the snipping tool
Mac: Shift + Command + 3 or + 4
Mac: use preview

For PC users, if you haven't yet discovered the Snipping Tool, I seriously suggest you take the time to find out about it. The newer version of Windows may have removed it (such a shame), but if you're working on an older computer it's probably there. Search on YouTube for *'where to find or how to use the snipping tool on Windows 7 or Windows 10'*. I think you'll like it!

Communication Channels

IT people tend to have their preferred communication channels and, as much as possible, you should stick to this. They're usually running task lists that are being updated and prioritised daily, and in some cases, hourly.

At DIY Digital, we prefer communication by email as we are able to include links to video tutorials or attach helpful cheat sheets specific to the issue, in our reply. We also manage our task list largely from our inbox. We also use phone calls when we need to ask our clients lots of questions and get real-time responses.

We don't like Facebook and text messages as they're often written too casually and they're less effective in being able to copy and paste links. They don't allow us to effectively manage our support help desk as we're unable to easily search by date, sender's name or subject.

Some IT businesses and online providers have systems for lodging support tickets. Don't let this phase you – give it a go.

If you have a social media agency, unlike us, they may insist on you using Facebook messages!

So, each agency is different and as much as possible I'd encourage you to try to relax into their communication mode.

Hands Free

If you're talking on the phone to your IT or website person, it's often useful to be hands free. They might ask you to click on something or navigate somewhere on your computer and it's difficult to do this if you've got a phone in your hands.

If you haven't already done so, learn how to use the speaker on your phone so you can talk hands-free. Or alternatively be part of the in-crowd and start using a headset.

Desktop (not phone) for Business Administration

For business administration and management purposes use a desktop, not a tablet or phone. Settings tend to be harder to find on the smaller devices. Smartphones are great for recreational use but keep to the desktops or laptops for business.

Remote Screen Support

Sometimes your website developer or IT person may wish to use screen share devices such as Zoom or TeamViewer. These are great tools for not only support, but also online meetings, coaching and consulting.

If you've never used these before, let the person on the other end know it's your first time. This way, they're likely to guide you through the process. If you don't tell them it's your first time, they're likely to assume you're comfortable with the technology and ready to go. This means they might go too fast and leave you behind.

Logging In and Logging Out

Sometimes logging or signing out of the system will solve a problem. Have a cup of tea. Maybe the internet connection is just playing up for a little while. Go back to it when you're ready.

Ctrl Alt Delete

When you're working on a computer and your program freezes, use the Ctrl + Alt + Delete keys all at the same time (or Command + Option + Escape on a Mac) and this will bring up a window that shows all the programs that are running. From this window you can shut down any of the programs, including the one that's frozen.

Although you'll lose any unsaved work, sometimes it's the only way.

Turn It Off and On Again

Cliché – but true! Sometimes turning the program, or the computer or modem or router or other piece of machinery, off and on again does work.

Log out of everything. Turn the computer off (sometimes you'll need to hold the power button down for 6 seconds), walk away for 5 minutes and then turn it on again.

Learn the Basics

Many baby boomers missed out on learning the basics of how computers and software work. Many older workers in an office environment accidentally, and almost imperceptibly, learnt how to use a computer little by little – one question one day, another question another day – before long they had a good understanding. However, if you've worked most of your life outside an office environment (e.g. nurses and tradies) you're likely to have missed out on a lot of the on-the-job computer learning and had to learn most of it on your own. This is the tough way of doing it.

Not knowing the basics is a common problem between IT consultants and their older clients.

Imagine trying to teach someone to cook if they don't know what 'sauté' means. Let's say they resist learning the jargon and get upset with you when you use the word as they don't understand it and resent having to learn it. Most cookbooks refer to the process of cooking onion and garlic in a small amount of hot oil until they are transparent as 'sauté the onion and garlic'. It's going to be a pretty frustrating process working with someone who resents the word 'sauté' being used if you're teaching them to cook, isn't it? That's how your IT person or website developer feels if there is a continued resistance to learn the basics and the language of computer navigation.

There are some great government programs available to older Australians to assist them with computers. There are also a lot of private operators who offer classes and one-on-one teaching.

Learning the basics will lead to less things going wrong. It won't stop things going wrong – that will still happen – but it will lessen the amount of times it happens and enable you to deal with it better when it does.

Contracts, Agreements and Service Provision

The number of communication breakdowns, upset clients and frustrated IT providers is significant. Our industry needs to pull up its socks.

Having said that, I'm amazed by the number of small business owners who sign contracts for websites or online marketing services that they don't understand.

Two things to ask are:

- what am I not getting?
- what are the alternatives?

These two questions will help you nail down the key elements of what you are purchasing.

Spreading the Love or Spreading the Frustration

Getting frustrated with computers and online platforms is common. If you're frustrated or emotional about the situation, take a deep breath, have a cup of tea and give it 24 hours. When you're calm, give your IT support person a call.

IT problems may happen because the IT person didn't do something right, but it might be because the software has been updated and is no longer playing nicely with the set-up. Maybe it's because Google or Facebook changed something and it's affected everyone. Maybe your internet connection is slow. Maybe you've accidentally ticked the wrong check box. Maybe it isn't in the contract for the IT person to provide.

More often than not, it's not until the problem has been solved that the reason for it going wrong can be known. Jumping to conclusions that it's the IT person's fault, if that is what you have done, may be unfair.

If you would hesitate to say something face-to-face, don't write it in an email. Pick up the phone and sort out the issue as best you can with a real-time, civil conversation.

Keep the relationship with your IT, website and other suppliers and consultants in good shape. Your mental health, and theirs, is important.

Things going wrong is a very good reason to not leave things until the last minute when dealing with techy stuff. Technology can, and often does, go wrong. Leave plenty of time to allow for stuff to go wrong. With no looming deadline, you're much more likely to deal with the situation in a better frame of mind.

Next Steps – What you can do

Create a recording system that works for you. One where you'll be able to find your usernames and passwords.

Learn how to take a screenshot.

Learn what a URL is (it's a web address), how to copy it and how to paste it into an email.

Find out the name of the browser you regularly use. Write down the name of the computer you are using and how to find the name and version of the software you regularly work on.

Practice being ok with lodging support tickets online.

Learn how to use your phone hands free.

Take a computer class if you need extra help or, if you prefer one-on-one training, Google '*one-on-one computer training in your city name*' and find out what help is available.

CHANNELS

CHAPTER 5

WEBSITE

In the first chapter I mentioned that putting time, effort and money into your business website is important. For most businesses it should be considered as a high priority and one of the first online marketing tasks to be implemented.

In this chapter we'll talk about where some of those efforts should be focused. This applies when you are first developing your website, or if you feel your site needs a makeover.

Website Size

How many pages does your website have?

In the SEO chapter, I talk about how the more pages you have the easier it is to optimise for search engines. However, a one-page site is really easy to scroll, and fantastic for mobile phones.

So, you have to make a decision – do you want to have a highly informative site with lots of pages – or a super mobile-friendly, easy to scroll one-page site?

The more complicated your service, or the more niche it is, the more you'll need to explain yourself. You may need lots of information for people to read and thereby understand what your product or service is all about.

For example, if you are an engineering firm providing additive machining and component supplies you'll need a few pages to explain this speciality.

However, if you're a plumber, hairdresser, physiotherapist or other well-known household service, you could get away with a one-page super mobile-friendly site, as most people understand these services. But you will find it hard to optimise. If you want to optimise a site like this you might need to consider writing blog articles or consider promoting your site with Google Ads instead of, or in addition to, SEO.

Next Steps – What you can do

If you haven't yet got a website for your business, consider whether simplicity is right for you or a more informative site is a better fit.

If you've already got a website, take a good look at it. Can you get away with it being a one-page super mobile-friendly site or do you need to use plenty of pages to be informative?

Website Navigation

If you add more pages, you need to think very carefully about what pages you have. You might not get this correct at the start-up stage. It may take 2 or 3 years before you understand what your customers are asking for and what services are popular. You need to be able to adjust your website as your business grows.

Think about how people navigate to the pages and what you're going to name them. Go back to your customer profile. What would they need? What would help them?

The hierarchy of website pages is important for the person who comes to your site. It's also important for search engine optimisation. Be clear. Be very clear. Don't be messy and don't be complicated. Try to make it very easy to understand. This is often harder to achieve than it sounds.

A slight feeling on your part that the site isn't quite right indicates your site is not good enough. Business owners tend to downplay the problems on their website. I'm not sure why this is, but mostly I find business owners are not harsh enough critics of their own site. Be critical! The impression your business creates from your website can be the difference between getting a phone call or not hearing from a prospect. People dismiss a website very quickly, much more quickly than they dismiss you if you are talking with them face-to-face. Most people do not linger and read a website in a leisurely fashion. They take a brief look and make a quick decision as to whether to stay or go. Most of them go.

Your online presence needs to be simple, accurate and authentic.

Next Steps – What you can do

Click or tap through every page on your website. Does the way you move from one page to another make sense? Are the most important pages seen in the top menu? Read the text on the page – does the name of the page summarise what's written on the page?

Website Conversion

What do you want a person who comes to your website to do beyond reading the information?

Do you want the person to:

- make an enquiry
- book a demonstration
- sign up to your newsletter
- phone you, or
- ask you for a quote?

All these things are similar, but slightly different. These small differences are important when designing the site and allocating what messages get priority.

Ask yourself:

- Would you really like them to pick up the phone and make an enquiry?
- Would you really like them to fill in that form and book a demo?
- Would you really like them to book an appointment?

Think about the most important thing you want the person who comes to your website to do, other than read the information on it. What is your top priority? That's called the call-to-action. It's vital that you make whatever is the most important thing you want them to do super clear. You need to give it prominence on the homepage and perhaps even put it in the header so that it appears on every page. Often the call-to-action will be a button or a small coloured box that the website visitor can click on.

And here's the scary part — it's almost always better to have only one call-to-action – and certainly no more than two.

Next Steps – What you can do

Decide on your call-to-action.

Look at your homepage. Is the call-to-action clearly seen? If not, update your homepage so your website visitor is encouraged to call you or make an enquiry or whatever your top priority call-to-action is.

Information on Website

What information are you going to include, or not include, on your website? This can be a difficult process for some business owners. Think about your first-time customer or your customer profile. This pretend person is going to help you write content for your website.

One of the tricks you can use to write good content for your website is to pretend you're starting your business from scratch. Go back to the day when you were launching your business. It was a pretty exciting time in your life wasn't it? So, you've made the decision to start your own business, you remember that feeling of excitement mixed in with being a little bit nervous.

Now pretend a family member, who you haven't seen for a while, is visiting from interstate. You don't see them that often, but they're about to come over and you're about to launch your business. You've got some exciting news to tell them and that exciting news is that you're going to start a business.

Write your website content as if you're describing your business to this relative. This is a trick you can use to inspire and focus your writing on what matters.

Once you've got the bulk of the content written, edit it and refine it.

Next Steps – What you can do

Ask someone you know, who you trust to do the task, to read the main pages of your website and give you feedback. Ask two or three people. In the end, trust your own judgement, but do listen to what other people say – it might be enlightening.

If you can, hire a copywriter to look over your text and update it. They'll give you that competitive edge.

Website Images

Images are very important on websites. As they say, a picture paints a thousand words, and with websites this is absolutely true.

Images for websites need to be good quality. This means they need to be in focus, well lit and framed well. The images need to be better quality than the images you use on Facebook.

Ensure the photos you use do not contravene copyright.

As much as possible photos need to be real, authentic photos of you and your business, your building, your tools and your team. These will nearly always be better than stock images. Whenever you can, get real images. Spending time on getting good images is time well spent.

Examples of real business photos are:

- photos of your premises (inside and outside)
- photos of yourself or staff
  - professionally taken head shots
  - using a computer
  - using machinery
  - on the phone
  - beside the work car, if it has your business name sign written on it
  - beside a banner or sign with your business name printed on it
  - at an expo, fair or trade show
  - out and about networking
  - action shot at work
  - shelving with product on it

    - in work clothes holding a typical tool used in your line of work
- photos of a customer looking at a product, using your product or talking with you

It can be hard to get good images for your website, but it's well worth the time and money you spend to do so. It will make a world of difference to the trust that visitors to your site will have in your business. If the business feels trustworthy they are much more likely to pick up the phone and call you.

Having said that, sometimes it's just not possible to get authentic photos. In this case use stock images. There are many sites that sell non-copyright and royalty-free images – these are called stock images sites. Some are free, some cost between $5 and $20 a photo.

Although you can get stock images, I don't encourage it. People can smell a rat and they kind of know it's not really your business. It makes them a bit wary of you and you don't want people to be wary of you when they go to your website. You want them to trust you.

Next Steps – What you can do

Does your website look a little cold or remote? If so, it might be the images. Do you have real images from your own business or are you using stock images?

If your images could be improved, set yourself a 3-month goal to add new ones.

Website Technology

Website technology is where many business owners get confused as there is so much information it can be hard to understand what's important to know and what can be ignored.

In the 90s and 2000s, website developers very much came from the IT industry. Most websites were built using code. In other words, you needed this specialist skill to build them and, in many cases, maintain them.

Now there are oodles of platforms available to both website developers and non-developers to build a website. In our DIY chapter we've talked about some of the key considerations with different platforms.

There are 5 key items that are handy to understand when it comes to website technology:

1. Domain name
2. Hosting
3. Website builder
4. Themes
5. Plug-ins or add-ons

Domain Name

A domain name is your master web address. It's the bit that comes after the www or more commonly now, the https://.

For example, if your website is https://abcconsultancy.com, your domain name is abcconsultancy.com. You may have other pages on your website, for example

- abcconsultancy.com/about

- abcconsultancy.com/prices
- abcconsultancy.com/services
- abcconsultancy.com/contact

But the master or main web address is abcconsultancy.com – and that is your domain name. Every website has one. And while it may be stating the obvious, you want it to be the same as your business name. If you choose a business name and the domain name is not available, you're in trouble. Purchase or register the two on the same day to ensure you get them both (and while you're at it secure your Facebook Business Page name as well).

The web address gets called the domain name when you purchase it. It almost never gets called that again. Why the industry sought to make it a different name for the same thing, I'll never know.

In addition, you're also likely to come across the acronym URL. Essentially the URL is the web address as well. They're exactly the same thing – well almost – and we won't worry about the differences in this book. Usually a web address gets called a URL when you've hit a trouble spot and you're talking to an IT person.

So, a web address, at different times in its life, gets called a domain name or a URL. For the purposes of this book, to keep it simple, they're all the same thing.

Hosting

A website needs to sit on a computer somewhere in the world. That computer needs to be on 24/7, as customers expect to be able to access your site any time of the day or night. This computer is the host computer and the process is called hosting. It's best if the host computer is in a space that is flood-proof and fire-proof. Often this building is called a data centre. Sometimes the host computer is called a server.

The all-in-one website builders, such as Wix, Weebly, Squarespace and Shopify include hosting as part of their subscription fees.

Website builders, such as WordPress or Joomla, don't include hosting. Hosting needs to be purchased separately. It is harder to develop and maintain a website in builders that don't include hosting as part of their package, like WordPress, than it is for those that do include it, like Wix, as hosting is quite technical.

If you're purchasing your own hosting, you may not understand all the bits and pieces you're buying. You may end up paying for stuff you don't need, or not purchasing stuff that you later realise you do need. Often a developer will buy and arrange hosting on your behalf.

Website Builder

Examples of website builders are those already mentioned, e.g. Wix, Weebly, Squarespace, Shopify, WordPress and Joomla. There are lots of others. These are just some of the more popular ones.

Website Builders have replaced the need to have coding skills to build a website. Having said that, people with coding skills still use these skills to work at an advanced level within these builders. They can customise how the page looks or how the site functions using computer code.

The proprietary-branded website builders, such as Wix, Weebly, Squarespace and Shopify update their software without you ever realising it.

With platforms like Joomla and WordPress, the website manager needs to update the software. Occasionally an update will cause an error. Understanding who is responsible for updating your site, and at what cost, is one of the things to determine during your contract discussions with your website developer.

Researching which website platform or brand is best for you is time well spent. Think of it like you might if you're buying your child's first construction kit – will you buy LEGO® or Meccano? The purchase decision is not only based on what you want to immediately use, but is also made with a longer-term vision, knowing that once you buy a set, you're likely to stick with that brand for many years to come.

Usually you've invested a lot of time and learning into your website builder and it can be frustrating to lose that in a move to another platform. Research what you want from your website before you make a decision – it's worth it.

Themes

Themes connect with, and are integrated with, website builders. Each website builder will have its own collection of themes.

Themes are often grouped by industry or type of business. For example, there are themes for real estate agencies or cafes or hairdressers. Many do-it-yourself website developers like themes as it makes their job easier. Many professional website developers don't like themes as it restricts what they can do.

Plug-ins, Extensions, Modules or Apps

They get called different things by different website builders, but each website builder has its own collection of plug-ins (sometimes called extensions, modules or apps).

Plug-ins add that extra bit of functionality that doesn't come out of the box. Usually you have to pay extra. For example, if you buy a phone you expect it to be able to handle phone calls, send text messages and take photos. But if you want to have something that helps you with your daily fitness, you'd buy and download an app for that. That's what apps and plug-ins are with websites – that little bit extra that some people want, but not everyone.

Plug-ins, like themes and website builders, are all examples of software. Software needs to be updated as new versions come out. New versions fix bugs or add new features.

WordPress

WordPress is one of the most popular platforms being used. It's also the one that seems to get most business owners in hot water. For that reason, I'm giving it special mention in this book.

It has an interesting history. Back in 2003 a bunch of IT people said, '*We think we should make this website stuff available to the world for free.*' And they did! WordPress is open source software and is very good. They keep up with the times. There is a whole world-wide community around WordPress. There are literally thousands of themes and plugins that are designed to go with WordPress. Most of them work on what is called a freemium model. The basic version is free but you pay for the more sophisticated versions if you need to. Free + Premium = Freemium.

The open source nature of WordPress means there are hundreds and thousands of innovative and clever people writing software that is compatible with it. These pieces of software (i.e. themes, page-builders and plug-ins) are used by website developers to build WordPress sites.

WordPress is popular because it gives flexibility and functionality to website developers wanting to build a good site for a client.

Moving over to a new website developer is not a decision to take lightly. WordPress websites are built with different themes, plug-ins and modules. The person who built the site is likely to be very familiar with the plug-ins and software used, where-as another website developer may not be.

With flexibility and open source comes complexity. Let's use an analogy to help us understand how this impacts on your decision to hand over your WordPress site to a new developer.

What If Cars Were Made Using Open Source Designs?

Let's say there was an open source car maker. Let's say they made their car design available freely to the whole world – no patents, no legal stoushes over who owns what – just an incredible worldwide community that uses the basic car chassis design and adds to it as they see fit.

Now let's take it one step further and say that from the initial chassis design, lots of other car part designers came on board and made designs for car doors, windscreens, seats, locking devices, engines, radiators and braking systems. And these were also freely available to the worldwide community of car builders to use as they saw fit.

Somehow these car builders would need to make cars that were roadworthy, fit for purpose and complied with their country's road laws. And somehow, amazingly, it worked!

Wow – we'd get lots of interesting cars on the road, wouldn't we?

But how does this pan out for the car owner?

Let's say you're the proud owner of this roadworthy, law-compliant car and the brakes fail. You'd go back to the person or business that built the car and ask them to fix the brakes, or maybe the failure was prevented in the first place as you had a regular service schedule in place with them.

Our car example is somewhat of a hypothetical, but it's pretty close to the real situation if you're looking to get help with your WordPress site.

The reality is that your car door could have been designed in Belgium, the car braking system in Nepal and the air conditioning module in Australia. And although they all had free versions available, maybe the car maker decided to buy the premium version of the locking device so they could get particular features you had requested as well as accessing the support help desk if they needed to.

This happens in the world of WordPress. A website builder will buy a premium version of a plug-in to get features and access to the support team. Or they will purchase the plug-in from Belgium because they've used it before and they are familiar with how to install and configure it.

Does the plug-in from Belgium play nicely with the plug-in from Australia? Have those two software authors made them compatible with each other or, in the world of hundreds of thousands of WordPress plug-ins, have they not communicated with one another at all? Are both still in business and updating their plug-ins to be compatible with the latest versions of WordPress and website browsers?

WordPress Help

Choosing your website developer carefully, in the first instance, is a must to prevent a situation where you need to hand over your site. Choose a business you can trust to ensure your site is reliable and functional with a maintenance plan to prevent, or quickly address, errors.

Sticking with the person who developed your WordPress site is the best way of getting WordPress help. They know the website back to front and can easily move in and out of the various modules and parts to maintain and fix the site.

However, that sage advice is cold comfort if you find yourself in a situation where you need to move on from the original developer. Perhaps you had your site built overseas and would now prefer to communicate with someone local to you. Perhaps a friend built it for you and you've used up all the favours you feel you have. Perhaps you were working with a small business that has now gone out of business and is therefore no longer available to provide you with WordPress help.

Whatever the circumstances, you're now in the situation of needing help with your WordPress site.

Why Use WordPress at All?

This discussion naturally leads to why use WordPress at all if it's so much bother. That's a fair question and if you're building your own site the all-in-one commercial platforms such as Wix, Weebly or Squarespace may be the best choice for you.

Professional website developers want, and clients expect, sites to be built that look good and function well. The simpler builders, such as Wix, don't allow developers to meet the expectations clients have for their website. They restrict a lot of how the site can be designed. They have limited functionality. That's why so many developers use WordPress.

Next Steps – What you can do

Decide on the best website platform for you – don't leave it to chance or for someone else to decide for you. It's a major decision and impacts on what can and can't be done. Research the reasons for and against the various platforms.

Create, or revisit, your relationship with your website developer. Phone or face-to-face conversations will work best to repair any difficult scenarios. Be honest with them and hopefully they'll be honest in return. Have the conversation when you are in a good frame of mind and have plenty of time.

You don't need to know every bit of stuff about hosting, themes and plug-ins – but it is useful to understand the broad concepts as in this way you'll be able to talk with your website developer more easily.

Be honest with yourself, if you haven't paid the bills or if you accepted a contract or quote you didn't understand, it's possible it's not all the website developer's fault.

Be aware the technology changes quickly. If you leave it years between updating software or attending to the problem, it can exacerbate the situation.

TEMPLATE

Questions for Website Developer

How many websites have you built?

What is your experience in installing this piece of software?

What exactly does the service agreement cover?

What doesn't the service agreement cover that typically might be needed over the course of having a website?

Are there any other alternatives?

What are the benefits of doing it this way?

What would happen if I don't do this?

Will I be able to edit and update my site myself?

What training do you provide to help me edit and update my site?

Where can I go to get training to help me edit and update my site?

If I update my site and something goes wrong, can you help me and at what cost?

If my site gets hacked or goes down, who's responsible for fixing it and at what cost, to restore it?

Case Study: Funeral and Life Memorial Celebrant — Website

Sole traders come in all colours, one of the more unique ones is a Funeral and Life Memorial Celebrant.

Trevor's journey into the world of digital marketing, by his own admission, has been slow. Many other celebrants have websites, but the industry does not particularly place a lot of emphasis on an online presence. Personal reputation is everything.

After some time, Trevor created a LinkedIn profile and regularly posted on it. A little while later he established a Facebook presence.

Later down the track he was speaking with a business advisor who suggested he would not be seen as a credible business without a website. It was at that point Trevor decided he would get a website.

For Trevor it was important his site was not a 'look at me' site, but more an answer to families who were enduring incredible sorrow due to loss.

Trevor has found it very beneficial to hand his card to people and direct them to his website for more information. It's from the website that families can get a sense of who he is and the services he offers.

When the site went live, Trevor called himself a Funeral Celebrant. After market research he changed this to Life Memorial and Funeral Celebrant. His emphasis being more on the celebration of life, together with the sensitivity families require at these times. The word funeral was maintained for SEO purposes.

One of the good things about websites, unlike printed brochures, is that they can be updated in real time to take into consideration new strategies, branding and services.

Trevor is also an active blogger. Most of his articles began on Google Plus, but with the closure of that channel, his website became his digital home. It's the base from which most other strategies, including social media, flow. Google is 'king' of online presence and having a website allows you to be there first.

For Trevor, the more access points and communication channels he can be seen on, and be 'front of mind' when the need arises, the more likely it is that people will call him for assistance in their time of need.

Although many people might not like to speak about grief, dying and funerals, it is a service we all need at some stage.

CHAPTER 6

SEO

Search Engine Optimisation, or SEO, is the range of techniques used to get a website found on page one of a Google search.

Google is a search engine. Other search engines are Yahoo and Bing, but Google is the big one, so we'll refer to Google in this book.

If you are selling products on eBay, Amazon or Etsy, or you are using online directories like Airbnb or hipages, you can liken how their search works to search engine optimisation as well. Similar principles apply – you want to be found amongst a list of other competing businesses from a catalogue of choices.

It can take six months and even up to three years for optimisation to get results, so SEO is a long-term commitment and strategy.

Google Ads, that is, paying money directly to Google, can also be used to get your website found on page one. This will get results much quicker than SEO and take a lot less effort. However, Search Engine Optimisation will tend to keep working beyond its initial implementation, whereas advertising will stop working the minute you stop paying for it. Basically, Google Ads is the quick fix and SEO is the long haul.

Google search results can be likened to the results of looking for a book using an online library catalogue. Let's think about when a person goes into a library and searches for a book using the library's computer catalogue. Let's say they search for a book by John Smith.

If you're John Smith, and you want your book to be read by library visitors, the first thing you've got to have is the book. The book's got to exist and be in the library collection. In other words, for your website to come up in search engines you have to have a website and then Google has to know that it exists.

Let's say those two things have been accomplished. Will John Smith come up in your search?

This is a highly competitive space because John Smith is a very popular name. There might be 30 books that are authored by John Smith in this library. Yet the results page of your library search only lists 10 books per screen.

What if the person who's searching for the book in the library catalogue becomes a little more refined with their search. Let's say they search *John Smith gardening* because it's a gardening book they're after. Maybe the book comes up, maybe not. Maybe there's still a lot of John Smiths who do gardening books.

Let's say the person gets even more refined in their search and they search for *John Smith gardening native plants in Australia*. Now it will definitely come up.

The library catalogue is searching for the best match. This is exactly what Google is doing. Google is searching for the best match. If it thinks your website is the best match, you will get the number one spot. If it thinks your competitor is the best match, they will get the number one spot and not you.

So, when we talk about Google searches we're talking about getting the best match for a search term that somebody is searching for.

Let's consider another example. Let's say the person searching the library catalogue doesn't know that John Smith is the author of a gardening book about native plants in Australia. In this instance they don't search for John Smith at all.

They might search for something like *gardening native plants in Australia*. So that's a different search term and a more competitive space for authors, as the library catalogue doesn't have that extra clue of the author's name. If you're the author, you're now competing with every other author in your field.

In this example the author's name is like your business name. If somebody knows your business name, they're likely to Google your business name. Chances are, you come up number one on Google for your business name, and I hope you do.

But what if they don't know your business name? They just know the type of business they're looking for? They're looking for a physio or handmade birthday cards or holiday rental accommodation places.

In this instance, you're competing with every other business similar to yours.

To get ahead of your competitors in the search results, you have to give Google all the clues you possibly can. And these clues are what's called optimisation techniques. Every little bit of optimisation activity is another clue.

The more clues you have, and the better quality those clues are, the more you'll win in the SEO space.

And the more astutely you are tuned into what phrase a person will search for, that is relevant to your business, the more you'll win in the SEO space.

Next Steps – What you can do

Think about what searches people could use to find you. You've probably already worked out what the most obvious one is, but what about others? Think back to your customer profile – what might they search for? Think back to the first time a customer was looking for your product, the time when they didn't really know what it might be called in the industry. Think about what problem they are trying to solve or what situation they are in.

Many business owners find the concept of search terms (also called keywords) too difficult or irrelevant to their work. However, understanding this can give you the competitive edge. Open up to how people might search for you. From when they're first thinking about an idea, right through to when they are searching for a specific product or service and they are ready to make a purchase. The phrases they use are likely to be different depending on where they are in the decision-making process.

Is your business attracting potential clients or customers through a good understanding of how they might find you online, or are you missing out? Brainstorm with staff, friends and colleagues for inspiration and ideas.

TEMPLATE
Search Terms

Search Term One: My Business Name

☐ Yes, I come up on page one of Google on my business name

☐ No, I don't come up on page one of Google on my business name

Search Term Two:

☐ Yes, I come up on page one of Google on search term two

☐ No, I don't come up on page one of Google on search term two

Search Term Three:

☐ Yes, I come up on page one of Google on search term three

☐ No, I don't come up on page one of Google on search term three

There is no silver bullet. There isn't just one thing you can do that will guarantee you optimisation success. It doesn't happen like that. Activities for a committed SEO strategy include link-building, writing lots of information and concentrating on the technical health of your website. There's a range of techniques. You can employ all of them or some of them.

Search Engine Optimisation is a complicated area and takes time and effort to learn. People who specialise in this field are keeping up with ever-changing trends and are highly sought after for their expertise. That's why, if you're outsourcing this to the experts, it's expensive.

The good news is that doing something towards your SEO is likely to be helpful if you are in a relatively non-competitive space. Even if you're not perfect at it, if you're doing some optimisation activities, it's likely to have a helpful impact on your rankings.

In this book I'm not attempting to make you an expert. I'm listing a few techniques that can get you started.

The clues, or techniques, can be broadly placed into two categories:

1. technical, and
2. on-page or content.

Technical

Page Speed and Mobile Responsiveness are examples of optimisation techniques that would be considered technical.

Most people find it frustrating to wait for a website to load. Google ranks websites that load quickly better than websites that don't (all other things being equal). The time it takes a website to load is often called page speed. The benchmark for page speed is under three seconds. To fix a slow-loading website requires good technical knowledge and experience.

Lots of people search for and read websites on their phone. Google ranks websites that are mobile responsive better than websites that aren't (all other things being equal). The ease with which people can read a website equally well on a phone, tablet, laptop or desktop is called mobile responsiveness. Look at your own website on a phone and see if the text is too small to read or the links difficult to click on. In most cases, the fix for a site that isn't mobile responsive, especially if it is more than five years old, is to get a new website.

Next Steps – What you can do

Look at your website on a mobile phone. Can you read the text without pinching and zooming? Click on the links and buttons – are they easy to click on – or do other things overlap too much?

Having a website that doesn't work on a mobile phone is no longer an option.

Content or On-Page SEO

If you have a one-page website, that is you've got the home or front page and no other pages, it will be hard for you to optimise your site using content as a technique. Content or on-page SEO works great for:

- businesses with a multiple service pages, each one describing a unique service
- online shops
- websites with active blog articles or news updates.

Service Pages

If you have service pages, and you've got different pages for each type of service, then you'll be able to optimise using this technique. The aim is to write at least 300 words per service page. Clear, easy, informative writing that gives the visitor to your website an excellent understanding of how your service helps solve their problem.

Product Pages

If you have an e-commerce store, and you have products that people can buy online, this technique will work for you, however it's very hard to write 300 words on a product page. It starts sounding like you're waffling on, and you probably are. Aim for 150 words.

One trick online shops can use is to focus on the category or collection pages. In an online shop the category page usually gives you the best chance of writing 300 or more words. Think about those higher-level category pages as priority pages for your optimisation.

Blog Articles or News Items

Content SEO is particularly beneficial if you write articles as part of a blog or regularly update your site with news articles.

If you have a one-page site, and you've identified SEO as one of your strategically important marketing activities, you may need to consider starting a blog.

A blog is a collection of articles that are written on a website. It's a bit like a journal the author makes available to the public to read. It will usually have a theme related to the business. For example, a business consultant might write about leadership or a wellness coach might have a healthy recipes blog.

Blog articles are a great way of optimising your site as they have a lot of text and Google loves text. Text holds a lot of clues for Google's bots to read. I'm not sure why they're called Google bots – maybe its short for robots – at any rate, Google has a way of automatically reading the text on websites.

In addition to giving Google lots of clues, blog articles can be super useful in a number of different ways, for example:

- to provide content for your social media by posting about, and linking to, the articles
- to use as support pages for your customers by answering common questions
- to gain authority in your space by demonstrating your expertise in your industry
- to test and clarify your own ideas in your field

Tricks of the Trade

The general rule of thumb is to optimise one page per search term. This is why content SEO as a technique is hard to apply to one-page sites, as they only have the one page to optimise.

A search term also gets called a keyword. The easiest way for beginners to start with SEO is to optimise one page per keyword. Keyword is a misleading term because most often it's a 'key phrase', three or four words, but in the industry it gets called a keyword.

Keyphrase, or keyword, is exactly the same thing as a search term. In other words, in our example of the native gardening book, *gardening native plants in Australia* is five words, so that's the keyword. That's what somebody is searching for in the catalogue, or search engine. The search term is the key phrase, which is the keyword – they're all the same thing!

For beginners, the best way to think about on-page or content SEO, is one search term per web page.

Keyword Research

Most search terms are obvious, but some aren't, and those that are really obvious are often already used by your competitors.

And in any case, even though you know, or think you know, the best search terms, you won't know how many people search for that term unless you do keyword research. Keyword research gives you search volume and other insights that are very helpful when optimising your pages.

With regard to search terms, quality (i.e. relevance to your business) and quantity matter.

Once you've decided on your search term, write or update the page with that search term in mind. Write 300 words or more and add the search term into the writing three times.

By doing this, you are giving Google clues about what the page is about. By repeating the search term on the page, Google gets the point that this page is particularly important for that term.

Other neat tricks that will enhance the importance of the keyword are:

- use the search term in the heading
- have the search term as the page title
- use bold typeface for one instance of the search term

Next Steps – What you can do

Pick your three most important pages. Prioritise those and optimise each one of them. Once you've done your top three, work through the next three.

Links

Another thing that can help your site rank better on Google is links.

If another website mentions your business, and links back to your website, that is a link (or a backlink or hyperlink) and it's very good for your Search Engine Optimisation.

For example, local business associations often have a directory of their members on their website. The directory listing usually includes the business name, two or three sentences about the business, phone number and website. When somebody clicks on the website entry, they are taken to the member's website. That's a backlink or a link.

If you're trying to find ways to get links back to your site, you might consider joining your local business association.

If you write an article that is published on another website, there could be a link from their site to yours. In these situations, there will usually be a guest author bio with a photo, two or three sentences about the author and the author's website. Sometimes you can get links by writing articles on other people's sites.

Linking from your site to other sites will also help with your Search Engine Optimisation. For example, if you have a health related site and there's a government website that has information about local health services, you might wish to link to that site from your site. By doing this you are demonstrating to Google that you're being helpful and connecting people to information of interest. Google rewards you for this helpfulness by allocating you a few extra SEO points.

Two Other Things

Two other things on SEO before we leave are:

1. the age of your website, and
2. the freshness of your content.

All other things being equal, if your competitor's website has been around for five years longer than yours, they're likely to rank better. They've had a lot of people go to their website in those five years, hence the site has some authority in Google's view. If you've just got your website live in the last few months, it will take time to get your site to rank well.

If you have an old website, but you've let it languish for five years, Google will know this and not like it. Google rewards websites that are being updated with fresh content. Update the content every now and then, at least every couple of months.

The good news is that for businesses in a low to medium competitive environment, you can do some basic Search Engine Optimisation and it's likely to have a good, long-term positive impact on your business.

Writing content on your website is a good tactic – but writing content takes time and isn't for everyone. Four to five hours every month is very likely to generate results. Think of it as being the tortoise rather than the hare.

The above provides a simple guide on how to optimise your website pages for search engines. There's a lot more we could add in, for example clean coding, duplicate content, readability and lots more. If SEO is an important marketing strategy for you, I encourage you to read more beyond my brief guide here.

Next Steps – What you can do

Pick a page you'd like to optimise and work through the process as best you can. Don't try to learn and implement all of the possible SEO techniques in one go – it's a complicated area and best approached bit by bit. Try to learn some of the jargon (there's a lot!) as you go.

There is no silver bullet.

If you find that your writing becomes stilted and odd because you start writing for Google's bots, rather than for a real human being, stop. The real person comes first. If you need to trade off not having a keyword in a heading, or only writing it two times in the article, do that. The over-arching rule is that Google wants to reward websites that are informative and interesting to the user. First and foremost, write good content. Use the techniques if you can, but let them go if you can't.

Feel free to visit diydigital.com.au and contact us about our do-it-yourself SEO packages.

Case Study: Online Skincare Shop — SEO

An online shop sells skincare products, including shampoo. There are two types of shampoo – lavender and aloe vera.

There is a product page for lavender shampoo and there's a product page for aloe vera shampoo. Each shampoo has a distinct page and therefore each one can be optimised, distinct from the other. Each shampoo page can be optimised for a different search term.

The easy thing to do would be to optimise the aloe vera shampoo for the search term *aloe vera shampoo* and the lavender shampoo for *lavender shampoo*. However, this might not reach the broadest number of possible buyers.

A more valuable strategy might be to optimise the aloe vera shampoo page on the search term *dandruff* and the lavender shampoo page for the search term *organic shampoo*.

Case Study: Lawyer — SEO

A lawyer in the city of Brisbane has a service page that talks about legal services they provide in the instance of a car accident, and another page which talks about the help they can give to a person who wants to make a workplace injury claim. Each of these are distinct service pages and can be optimised with their own distinct search term.

The search on *workplace injury Brisbane lawyer* is most likely the best search term for the service page that covers it. It's also the most likely search term every other lawyer in Brisbane is optimising their website for. As it is the best search term, this lawyer optimises their service page for it, with an expectation that they'll give it a go and hopefully it will eventually pay dividends.

In addition to having service pages, this lawyer writes blog articles. Three blog articles have been written pertaining to workplace injury:

» making a WorkSafe claim

» safety on construction sites

» quad bike accidents on farms

All three articles give the lawyer an opportunity to broaden the likelihood of their business being found on Google, by optimising the site beyond the most competitive and obvious search terms.

CHAPTER 7

SOCIAL MEDIA

We are living in the golden age of social media.

History will look back at this period and see that it was the land of plenty for the ability to reach consumers. We have so many social media and business marketing choices.

Simon Kingsnorth says in his textbook *Digital Marketing Strategy*, *"Social Media is a bit of a goliath these days – omnipresent, revered and lamented in equal doses, and most definitely misunderstood."* I couldn't agree with him more.

Some people love social media and are great at it.

Some businesses seem to be made for Facebook. For example, beauty, handicrafts, hobbies, pet services, kids' classes, fashion, fitness and travel.

Many tradies pick up jobs as a result of a neighbour or friend tagging or recommending them on Facebook.

However, many baby boomer business owners see Facebook only as a necessary evil sucking their time, rather than an opportunity they can get value from.

Many other small business owners mistakenly think that being on social media is essential and will generate interest in their products or services, just by being on it. You've got to be committed on these channels to really make an impact. There are plenty of seminars, workshops, articles and videos available to learn about social media and there are lots of different ways to do it well. Business owners can create, and own, their own voice. This can be fun and energising. This is one task that doesn't need to be outsourced to the experts but, if this is your pick, don't get lazy or complacent.

It doesn't make sense to have a social media presence when it isn't getting you a return on investment or return on time. If this is what you feel is happening with your social media, consider using a housekeeping strategy. Under a housekeeping strategy, you might do a post once a week. Just post often enough that people know you're still in business, don't over-resource it.

But for those of you who really love your social media, really hit it out of the ballpark – because this is the golden age of social media.

Social media is a great marketing option that wasn't available to businesses in the 70s, 80s and 90s. Learn about live streaming, creating groups, connecting with or tagging people, commenting on other people's posts and all the other capabilities the channels give you.

"... if a post is deemed uninteresting, it will reach just a tiny part of the potential audience. Engaging content is pushed to the top, and uninteresting content is not even shown in the News Feed. Attention on Facebook has to be earned." Clo Willaerts.

For many business owners, finding great content for their social media channels is their biggest challenge. The following is provided to help inspire you to find great content:

Facebook Post Ideas

1. Products and services
2. New stuff
3. Discounts and specials
4. Events
5. People
6. Behind the scenes
7. Unique you
8. The boring stuff
9. Testimonials and reviews
10. Your website
11. Hints 'n' tips
12. Weird and wonderful
13. The outside world

Products and Services

This one is pretty straightforward. Use your Facebook page to promote the products you sell or the services you offer. Don't do this for every post. Occasionally sprinkle this in amongst other content.

New Stuff

- Launches
- New releases
- New products
- New ways of delivering your service

Most business owners are great at announcing new stuff on Facebook. In fact, many do it to the exclusion of other posts. Facebook is a great place to announce new things that are happening in your business. So, keep doing it!

Have We Got a Deal For You

- Discount offers
- Weekend specials
- Season specials

Here's another Facebook Post that most business owners are great at – keep doing it, you're on the right track!

Events

If you're running, or attending, seminars, workshops, trade-only days or a back-to-school event, make sure to promote it on your business Facebook page. In fact, you may wish to create an event just to get people talking. Here are a few examples:

- Conferences
- Seminars
- Trade days
- Come 'n' try days
- Charity day
- Father's Day

Don't restrict it to events you're organising, be sure to include those events you are attending. People love to hear about what you are up to and how you are keeping up with knowledge in your area of expertise.

People at Work

- Tradies at work
- Happy customers
- Warehouse team members

Many business owners significantly underestimate how much people enjoy seeing you, your staff and your customers. Get photos. If possible, get videos. You don't need to win photography awards – but have the photo in focus and, if posting a video, ensure the sound is good – or off.

Behind the Scenes

- How do you make the product?
- How do you identify the problems?
- What special ingredients or methods do you use?
- How long does it take?

Many business owners significantly underestimate how much people enjoy learning about what you do and how you do it. Allow your customers a sneak-peek into how your industry works – it's surprisingly fascinating for many.

Unique You

- Niche products that only you stock
- a special service hardly anyone else provides
- special deliveries you do that others don't
- custom-made or sourced items
- personalised gift cards

Many small business owners start their business because they've found a niche in the market that other bigger, less nimble businesses are unable to supply or haven't identified. However, five years down the track, this is often forgotten in the hubbub of making the business work. This information makes for great social media content. Go back to where the passion for your business started – and talk about this on your social media pages.

The Boring Stuff

Every now and again, not too often, remind your loyal fans about:

- your opening hours
- the warranty on your products or services
- the personal service you offer
- where you are located

Many business owners forget to sometimes just let people know what they do. While this isn't recommended to be a regular social media post, because it might be a little dull, every now and then it's appropriate. Use a background colour, graphic or photo to help 'zhoosh' this one up.

Testimonials and Reviews

If a client or customer has given you a five-star review, be sure to take a screen shot and post it in your main newsfeed to ensure everyone gets to hear about it. Milk it for all it's worth!

Website

Your website is the window to your business. Regardless of the newsfeed cycle of Facebook and its algorithms, your website is a place your customers can go and know they are getting the whole picture of who you are and what your business does. Linking to your website from Facebook is an important post, and most businesses should look to do this at least once a fortnight. Provide a brief one or two sentence summary and link to:

- an online product
- a page describing your services
- your Homepage
- blog articles

Many business owners forget to do this. Add this one to your bag of tricks.

Hints 'n' Tips

If you're an accountant, lawyer or other professional who provides a service based on your knowledge and expertise, sharing some of that expertise in a simple, friendly way on your social media channels builds trust. For example, a bookkeeping tip if you are an accountant or advice on the first thing to do if you are in a car accident, if you are a lawyer. A short, educational piece that is generally helpful.

Tradies, in particular, have a wealth of knowledge they can share. Think about what you wish your customers would know, or do, before they called you. For example, if you're a tiler you may want the customer to measure the space to be tiled before calling you, so at least you have a rough idea of the size of the job. If this is the case, create a post or video about how to measure a floor or wall area. This is a great hint to give your customers.

The Weird and Wonderful

Facebook loves the weird and wonderful – look up board games, quiz night questions or crossword puzzles for inspiration. You'll find a wealth of odd-ball ideas which may inspire your next Facebook post. For example, if you are a dietician you might post about tongue prints, like fingerprints, being different for everyone. Or if you sell honey, you can share the fun fact that sometimes when they're out gathering nectar, bees will fall asleep in flowers.

The Outside World

Informing your clients and customers about what is happening in your industry lets them know you're keeping up with trends and best practices in your area of expertise. Posts might be:

- interesting articles written by like experts in another country or state
- government or industry updates in your area (if not too technical)
- a news item with your view of the story

It can be hard to keep these fun and interesting, and social media works best with fun and interesting. So not too often, but don't let this languish to never. Keep it short and simple.

Snippets not Stories

Social media is mostly about snippets and less about stories. If you're trying to tell a story you're possibly overestimating the staying power of Facebook users. Mostly they're just glancing through and having a peek.

Let's take an example. Let's say you're a carpenter and you want to do a 'behind-the-scenes' post. The post will be about putting a door into place. You're not posting about the whole process of how to put a door into place – you'll be doing a post about one small part of putting a door into place. Let's say there are five different hinge types to choose from, depending on what type of door it is. You might do a post about the five different hinge types or you might do a post about what hinge type you'd typically use on an indoor, light-weight wooden door. A photo of the hinge and the tool used to install it, or better still, a photo of the person putting the hinge in place. Or maybe you even create a 10-second video showing the hinge being installed.

Make your Facebook posts short, sharp and shiny snippets. Photos are a must. Videos are even better. Include faces and people in the photos and videos whenever you can.

TEMPLATE
13 Ideas Social Media Content

Feature product or service

Something new or being launched

Special or offer

Event I'm attending or an event I'm running

Photo of me or my staff

A behind the scenes snippet

Something unique about my business that other businesses like mine don't do

Our opening hours or warranty we provide or location

Customer testimonial or review

Website link

Hint or tip I can give my customers

Something odd, unusual, funny or interesting that's kind of relevant to the business

Something informative about the sector or industry we're in

Case Study: Hydro Excavation Company — Facebook

A Hydro Excavation company is not an entity that would typically be regarded as being trendy, or being the perfect business, to be on Facebook.

However, Natasha from South Vac Hydro has a presence on nearly every social media platform and finds that, for her, Facebook is the most successful.

Facebook does not generate new customers for the business, but it does nurture existing relationships and gives the business a small level of brand awareness in the local community.

On average, Natasha spends about one to three hours per week, depending on the amount of material she has available and level of creativity she has at the time!

She's trialled many different post subjects and concepts and feels the success for organic engagement (i.e. not advertisements, but posts added for free) is with personal posts. They have the most engagement with personal, non-sales stories.

For example, she will share a photo or video of the crew working on any unusual occurrence while they are on site (e.g. rain, wildlife or treasures they dig up!). She'll also share birthdays or personal achievements.

A popular post is a poll where people get to choose how their Monday is going, from two options. There is always a happy and sad option, with a sprinkle of humour and a corresponding photo of the crew on site.

Any storyline where the follower can personally connect seems to be the most popular.

Natasha spends much of her time reminding her team to send her photos of when they are out and about.

Natasha's Tips:

Don't use stock or internet photos. You don't have to be an expert photographer – people just need to connect with the image and story. Keep it real and be honest.

People are bombarded with enough advertising – you don't need to add a sales pitch to every post. Share stories about real people doing real things with the odd sprinkle of humour.

For a great example of a trade's Facebook page visit https://www.facebook.com/SouthVac/.

Case Study: Engineering Firm — LinkedIn

A small, but progressive, advanced manufacturing engineering firm, with large corporate clients in the government, rail and defence industries in Australia and the USA, uses LinkedIn to position the company and develop its brand.

The team members have been very strategic, determined and personable in using LinkedIn. The strategy is not only about what they do on this channel, it's also about what they don't do.

They focus on four key messages:

- they are user focused
- defence and rail experienced
- solve complex problems through their significant engineering experience
- offer a full, advanced manufacturing service

Each sales team member aims to do two posts a week. They do this to build credibility with existing clients and, to a lesser extent, develop new sales.

They only connect with people who they think they can do business with or who add credibility to their brand. In other words, they don't just connect with people for the sake of it. Each connection request is accompanied by a personal note and only made to people they've met at networking functions who have a strong connection with who they are, and what they do.

Interestingly, they have found LinkedIn a good way to connect with people in different departments, divisions or locations. Their clients are often big corporations with divisions and offices in different parts of the world. LinkedIn has assisted them in getting introductions to compatriots who work in different departments, cities or countries.

What they don't do is create casual or frivolous posts. They don't connect with people who are not related to the industries they work in.

They have found that lots of their clients, and many people in their industry, use LinkedIn.

Case Study: Online Fantasy Football League — Twitter

Fantasy Football is a competition where football fans choose a virtual team online, from real players, and earn points each week when those players perform well in real matches.

Nicole created a Fantasy Football League for Australian women's soccer in 2018. She and her team use Twitter to promote the website and their fantasy league.

Twitter is a social network very different from Facebook or Instagram. It's very much on the pulse. People are posting and reacting in real time to current affairs (for example sporting events, politics, celebrity news, new season TV shows). Trends on Twitter are rapid, unfiltered and usually short-lived. For the fantasy league team, this makes it the perfect medium to raise awareness for what they are doing. They time their posts around live women's football matches to catch the attention of people who are following those events. Simply using the hashtags of those events gets them into the feeds of their target market. Despite putting an equal (if not greater) effort into their Facebook marketing, it quickly became clear that Twitter was allowing them to reach more people, and specifically more people who would be interested in their website.

The content of their posts includes commentary on the football matches, discussing the form and performances of players, re-tweeting content from clubs, players and governing bodies and (of course) directing people to their website and fantasy league. Due to the periodic nature of relevant events, they don't need to be posting to

Twitter constantly. Tweets during matches tend to get the most interest but now that they've built up a reasonable following, they get far more engagement than they used to on their 'off-peak' tweets.

The most important thing is not how many tweets they do, or how frequently they tweet, but how timely those tweets are. They need to respond to events as quickly as their audience is (that is to say, immediately).

The most successful tweets are those that are both timely and insightful. They need to offer something new to the conversation – it isn't enough to simply repeat what others have already said. Having said that, re-tweeting and affirming others' content is looked upon favourably and helps to get reciprocating engagement from those people.

Nicole's Tips:

» Tweet during events that are relevant to your business

» Find and use the hashtags that people are using for those events

» Use images, videos, emojis and gifs to draw attention to your tweets

» Tag people if you are directly talking about them, or to them, in your tweet, but don't tag multiple, loosely related people (this is easily recognised by the Twitter audience as spam)

» Only use hashtags that are relevant to you – don't use a wide variety of hashtags just because they're trending (this is easily recognised as spam)

- » Re-tweet, like and comment on others' tweets in a positive way – this validation helps to improve your engagement with them and also helps you to appear in the feeds of their audience
- » Offer something new to the conversation
- » Respond to any comments as quickly as possible
- » Don't be afraid to joke and banter with people who interact with you on Twitter – it is a casual platform perfect for short, witty responses
- » Pin your important tweets (e.g. those directing people to your website) at the top of your profile so people will immediately see it when they click through

Visit sheplays.com.au or follow them on Twitter @sheplays_au.

References

Digital Marketing Strategy; an integrated approach to online marketing, by Simon Kingsnorth. 2nd Edition. Kogan Page publishers, UK. 2019.

Digital Marketing like a Pro; Prepare. Run. Optimise, by Clo Willaerts. Lannoo Campus Publishers, Belgium. 2018.

CHAPTER 8

OFF-LINE MARKETING

This book is about digital marketing, so it may seem odd to include a chapter about off-line marketing. But I can't help myself. The fact remains that word-of-mouth and face-to-face relationships are still much needed for businesses.

People trust people they've met. You don't get body language, voice clues or all those other rich relationship builders through online communication.

My recommendation is that one of the three key marketing activities you choose to commit time, money and resources to is one that allows you to meet people face-to-face.

Your activity might be:

- sponsoring or exhibiting at trade shows
- making phone calls
- attending networking events
- building a few key relationships and working on a referral basis

Your Key Message

Work on the key message you want to promote about your business. Practice it from time to time so that when the opportunity arises, you can easily let people know about the products you sell or the services you provide.

Often called an elevator pitch, your key message is what you might say to someone at a BBQ who asks you what you do. Can you explain your business in 30 seconds in such a way they will be interested or curious enough to ask you to tell them more?

Getting your key message right is quite hard for most of us. If you have an opportunity to speak with a business coach or advisor, talk about your key message with them, as it's beneficial to have someone else as a sounding board.

Face-to-face opportunities don't work in isolation of your online presence – many people will look up your website or look you up on LinkedIn or Facebook after they have met you.

There are many sweet spots where digital and off-line marketing work really well together.

Email and Networking

Email marketing works exceptionally well with a strong networking strategy.

At a typical chamber of commerce, business networking event or conference, a business owner may shake 20 hands, share their elevator pitch with 10 likely candidates and identify three to five people who might be interested in their services. Business cards will be exchanged with those three to five people.

Then what?

An excellent follow up is to add them to your newsletter list.

This follow up is the one that most businesses fail to do, yet it is very beneficial in getting the best long-term value from networking. Most small businesses fail to do this as they don't have a regular newsletter they send to their clients and their network.

For service professionals, working in the business-to-business environment, a regular newsletter is a great way to keep your business top of mind. Not only that, a good newsletter will demonstrate your expertise in your subject and industry.

Five minute conversations don't become personal connections unless that person gets to know you and trusts that you are a good business operator. Trust builds over time and with demonstrated evidence. By proactively keeping in contact with relevant information, the people you've networked with may become your clients.

Social Media and Referrals

Another example of digital and non-digital media complementing each other is how social media works well with referrals. Friends and neighbours are happy to tag tradies and house/family service businesses they've used and were happy with. From baby-sitting to lawn mowing to tiling the bathroom. If you're in this line of business, you want to consider having a solid Facebook page so that previous clients can refer you, if and when the time is right.

Website and Background Research

The classic example of how digital marketing works hand-in-hand with personal interactions is the website. People you've met can, and do, go to your website to research you and your business.

A good website will make you look professional. It will give you and your business credibility. If you don't have a website, those people you network with and have had business meetings with, are likely to think you're not successful or not serious. If your website looks clunky or badly designed, they may think the work you do will also be below standard.

Next Steps - What you can do

Work on your key message from your customer's point of view – what do they get? What problem do you solve for them? What delight will they receive from their purchase? Practice getting it to be 30 seconds. In this way you'll be ready for those networking opportunities when they arise.

Don't design your key message so that it describes everything you do. Design your key message so that it's likely to generate enough interest so that the listener asks you to tell them more.

TEMPLATE

Key Message or Elevator Pitch

Draft 1: Elevator Pitch

Time: .... Minutes .... seconds

Draft 2: Elevator Pitch

Time: .... Minutes .... seconds

Draft 3: Elevator Pitch

Time: .... seconds

☐ Yes, it's 30 seconds or under

Case Study: Aged Care Products — Traditional Selling with Online

David has run his own business or been in sales most of his working life. He understands how closing a sale works and what techniques to employ to showcase his products to best effect.

Recently, he purchased the rights to distribute a highly beneficial product to the aged care market in his state. This type of product traditionally requires a long lead time in decision making. There are many influencers on the purchase decision, from the CEO to the nursing staff to specialist health providers such as Occupational Therapists.

David understands that traditional marketing and sales work in concert with the digital space.

He knows that customers will tend to trust the person they speak with and then listen to what they are promoting. As he says, effective promotion is 7% words, 38% tone of voice and 55% body language, so backing up online efforts with face-to-face closing is important.

Brand recognition, key messaging, presenting Unique Selling Proposition benefits and closing sales with customers are all key ingredients to success and revenue growth.

David sees his digital and social media presence as working in conjunction with his face-to-face appointments in relaying business information. The website and online channels give an ability to highlight product features, benefits and price options to customers and potential clients.

He knows that his website can, and is likely to be, shared amongst the stakeholders. If he hasn't been able to meet personally with all of them, at least his online presence is available to all of them.

CHAPTER 9

EMAIL MARKETING

Email marketing is the poor cousin of social media.

We really are living in the golden age of social media, and as a result, lots of business owners have forgone email marketing in favour of social media. I'd encourage business owners to consider basic email marketing. By basic, I mean small lists with no email funnels or free giveaways. In other words, the easy way!

Many sole traders and small business owners also dismiss email marketing as they consider it to be spam.

By dismissing email marketing so readily, many businesses are missing out on a marketing channel that has very good return on investment. Time and time again, email outperforms other activities. It's a phenomenally good marketing tool and you can do it for next to no money and a small amount of learning.

Email marking doesn't have to be spam. In fact, it's very hard to get away with spam nowadays because of the significant enhancements to spam filters. Recent enhancements in spam filters by email providers such as Gmail and Outlook have significantly opened up opportunities for smaller players. Those businesses with lists of 5,000 and over, who sell heavily into their list using free giveaways, email funnels and other advanced techniques, are finding their emails being blocked by these filters. The big email providers such as Mailchimp and Infusionsoft are suspending accounts or limiting the ability for the large lists to operate. It was the Golden Age of email marketing but is no longer.

This means smaller businesses with lists of 200, 500 or 1,000, who are getting open rates of 25% or higher, are able to cut through where the bigger players are finding they're unable to.

Many small and micro businesses can benefit from email marketing.

I'd encourage you to think about beginning with a newsletter once a month. This works very well to keep your business top of mind.

If you are in a service industry, or high information industry, email marketing is a good fit. For example, lawyers, tax accountants, coaches and consultants – people who have information to share. Email marketing also works well for businesses that get clients through recommendations or referrals, as you're able to stay top of mind with those people who refer you.

If you're a gift shop, consider sending emails around Christmas and Mother's Day or use other seasonal timeframes rather than a regular newsletter. Setting the right tone and frequency for direct consumer emails is a little trickier than business to business emails.

For tradies or health professionals, an e-newsletter once every three months would be enough to keep you top of mind with your clients and customers.

With a small bed and breakfast business, most of your guests are first-time guests, with fewer repeat customers. Guests who have visited your wonderful part of the world are not likely to visit again. Therefore, email marketing is unlikely to be the best strategy for you.

Email marketing is highly beneficial in getting repeat business and nurturing current clients.

Very trendy at the moment, and you've probably seen this phrase, are email funnels. A marketing funnel is aimed at warming up cold leads. It's all about lead generation. Terms such as lead magnet or free e-books are often part of email funnels. We're not covering email funnels in this book as it's a more advanced technique (and as mentioned previously the larger lists built this way are decreasing in deliverability due to spam filters).

How to Avoid Spam

Spamming is when you send lots of emails to lots of people who don't want them.

That isn't the same as saying that nobody wants your emails!

What we want to do is send good emails, not too often, to the right people. If you do this, you will find email marketing will work for you and you won't be spamming.

If you send an email twice a week, some people on your list are likely to feel that is too often. If you send an email twice a month, most people on your list are probably going to think that's ok.

The frequency of your email schedule is important.

If you send an email to people who have no interest in your product or service, they're likely to feel you are spamming them.

If you send an email to people who have indicated an interest in your product or service, they're probably going to feel ok with that.

In other words, it's the relevance of the receiver who is on your list, that is important.

If you send stuff that is super sales pitchy, '*buy this now*', '*only in the next 24 hours*,' '*have I got a deal for you*' – that kind of stuff – at some point people will lose interest. This type of email will work once or twice, but not regularly. The tone of your email is important.

Get the frequency, relevance and tone right and you won't be spamming people.

Build Your List

The first thing to do is to build your list. You need to have email addresses for people who are interested in your business.

Current customers and clients should go on your list, that's number one.

If you meet people at networking events, add them.

The day after you meet them, send them a personal email, something along the lines of:

> *"Hey John, it was great to meet you last night. I've added you to my email list. I usually send a newsletter once a month packed with hints 'n' tips and news. Here's an example of one I sent last month. If this doesn't suit, please let me know and I'll unsubscribe you."*

No-one unsubscribes – not straight away anyway. They're too curious! Eventually some people will unsubscribe from your list, and you should give them that option, but very few people do to begin with.

A list is not a static thing you create once and then rely on it from then on. A list is dynamic – people go off the list and new people get on it.

Sometimes you meet people and forget to put them on, so give yourself a reminder every three months to clean up and tidy the list. Have your new clients been added? Have people you've quoted jobs for been added? Do a little bit of housekeeping with your list every now and again because lists are not static.

You've got to keep putting new people on the list. The list is the most important part of email marketing. Get it wrong and email marketing will fail. Get it right and you're over half-way to working this strategy.

Once you've got the list sorted, you can think about what to send them.

There are five emails I'd like you to consider:

1. Welcome newsletter
2. Monthly newsletter
3. Sales pitch/single issue
4. Surprise and delight
5. Annual unsubscribe email

Welcome Newsletter

This email is very basic. The structure is:

1. Welcome
2. How you came to be on this list
3. Photo of yourself, your team, your shop or similar
4. Unsubscribe, if you want to

Monthly Newsletter

This newsletter has two or three items of interest, or a story you'd like to share. If you are a counsellor or a self-help advisor in wellness, you might want to send them some helpful hints and tips or motivational quotes – something relevant to who you are and what your business provides.

If you've created a YouTube video or written a blog article, share that. If you have upcoming events, let your readers know about this. You can pop in a little advert about your upcoming class or retreat or your special service.

Sales Pitch/Single Issue

A few times a year you can play the trump card. This is the sales pitch email. If you do this too often your email marketing will be spam. But not doing it at all is too passive.

This sales pitch email works when it is a single issue email. Don't water the pitch down by hiding it amongst other newsletter items. Go for it! Make what you are selling the subject line and the only topic in the email.

For example, if you have a special on for the month of August, a half-price sale, or an important event coming up, this is the time to play this card.

Surprise and Delight

Occasionally send an email just for the delight of sharing something relevant about your business to your clients. No sales pitch. Nothing to buy, or register for, or spend money on. This will keep your clients and network interested in staying with you.

An example of a surprise and delight email is one that might have a fun fact related to your business, the opening of a new centre local to your area that is on topic for who you are, or insider's knowledge that you are able to talk about. Something that jumps out as being interesting, funny or highly informative that you are uniquely placed to share.

Annual Unsubscribe Email

The ability for people to unsubscribe will be in small font at the bottom of every email. However, I recommend creating this as an offer to the people on your list, once a year.

A new year unsubscribe email might look something like this:

> *"Happy New Year! We're excited to start the New Year with you.*
>
> *If you'd like to keep hearing about our upcoming activities and be motivated by our hints 'n' tips, stay tuned and let your inbox know this email address is not junk or spam.*
>
> *However if one of your New Year's resolutions is to streamline your inbox and we're on the bin list – you can unsubscribe here."*

1-2% of people will unsubscribe. Sad as it is to see them go, it's good for your list health and your email deliverability to only have people on the list who want to be on it.

It also builds trust for the other 98% who choose to stay on.

Next Steps — What you can do

Consider or reconsider if email marketing is right for you. It has a very good return on investment and a very good return on time. It's also technically one of the simpler digital marketing activities to conquer.

If you've already started with email marketing but lost your way, re-energise it. Make sure all your new contacts get added to the list and send them a nice welcome email.

If you've not yet started but want to, go ahead and build that list.

Fiona Blinco is an official partner with the Mailchimp Partner Program. Feel free to visit diydigital.com.au to find out more.

Case Study: Community Arts — Email Marketing

Leah regularly uses email newsletters to communicate with her local community about upcoming arts events. Managing art galleries means her mailing list is the best way for her to communicate with her audience.

Email compares differently with Facebook and other social media because she is able to target and tailor the message and communication to the audience. She has a mature audience who appreciate the slightly more formal email, rather than the broad net of social media.

Leah sends a monthly newsletter and feels this works well as it is a substantial email with plenty of images. In this age of masses of digital information, sending too often would turn some customers away. Occasionally something will come up outside of that cycle and when this happens she sends a special event email.

Compiling the email takes about two hours a month.

Every month the people on her list receive the annual arts program by pdf and the ability to book online using a button in the email.

Subscribing and unsubscribing is managed by the customer. Leah notices through the reports she receives that she has a reach of 300 more email addresses than the subscription list of 1200. From this she knows that her newsletters are shared on a regular basis.

Leah likes the professional polished look she can achieve with Mailchimp and how well it works with images. Switching to Mailchimp over a year ago has improved the quality of her communication with her audience considerably.

Leah's Tips

» I'd encourage you to use email to engage with your audience or customers on a regular, monthly basis

» keep adding new people to your list

CHAPTER 10

GOOGLE AND FACEBOOK ADVERTISING

There are many online advertising opportunities, for example Facebook, Google, YouTube, Instagram or LinkedIn. We'll focus on two:

1. Facebook advertising
2. Google advertising

Both platforms regularly change their look and features, and therefore it's hard to be too specific in a book as the details will change.

But let's take a look at the fundamentals:

The first thing most business owners will need to consider when they'd like to give online advertising a go is to choose whether they're going to use Google or Facebook.

If your products are fun, interesting, quirky, self-indulgent or similar, go for Facebook advertising. If you advertise with Facebook you can get your advert, including an image, in the newsfeed of your target audience.

If your product or service is practical, needed, important or similar, go for Google advertising. If you advertise on Google you can get your advert, including business name, two lines of text and a web link at the top of Google searches.

Considerations common to both are:

- location
- start and end dates
- set your maximum spend
- reporting
- small stuff is not small
- default settings

Location

With both platforms you can choose which suburbs, cities, towns or countries you want your ads to be seen in.

When computers are turned on they have what is called an IP address. This IP address identifies where the person who is operating the computer is located.

In other words, if you're using a computer in Sydney, Australia and a business has chosen to advertise their product in Sydney, you'll see it. If your sister is using a computer in Perth, Australia, she will not see it.

As a business you can choose where your advertisement shows.

Start and End Dates

With both Facebook and Google, you can choose specific dates for the adverts to start and finish.

Set Your Maximum Spend

You choose the maximum spend. The lowest would be $5/day. For larger businesses or go-getters it might be $100/day.

As an example, if you chose to spend $10/day from the 1st of July to the 10th of July, it would end up costing $100.

Reporting

Both platforms give you a report on how many times the ad was seen and how many times people clicked on it. The reporting takes time to understand, but once you do, it allows you to tweak and adjust the ads for best results.

Small Stuff is Not Small

Both Google and Facebook have what appears to first-timers as very small, insignificant checkboxes and options. Many of them are not insignificant. These things matter. What might seem like an insignificant tickbox choice is often not insignificant at all. There are lots of traps for new players and lots of ways for your money to be uselessly spent.

Default Settings

Both Google and Facebook have default settings and in both cases they're often more about getting more money for them, than they are about being strategically good advertising decisions for you. Buyer beware.

Google

Google advertising is a bit like SEO in that there are specialists in the field who keep up with the ever-changing trends and rules. It's unlikely you'll be able to run advanced Google ad campaigns without outside expertise. An advanced Google advertising campaign includes techniques such as re-marketing and regular optimisation.

Many small, local businesses don't need an advanced strategy. A basic Google advert can work quite well and generate leads for your business. Advanced campaigns are great and work well, but for local businesses they are often too much. If you can get enough new clients through the door with a basic advert, why pay a high monthly administration cost to get a more advanced advert you don't need?

There are lots of different types of Google ads but stick with the basic run-of-the-mill click-through to your website advert. This is often called getting traffic to your site and uses a Google text advert.

If you like working with numbers you'll be able to set-up and run your own Google ads. Getting help in the beginning will assist you in avoiding the many common mistakes.

Google has two advertising platforms:

- Smart Ads (formerly AdWords Express)
- Expert Mode

Google tends to draw newbies into the Smart Ads area. I don't recommend Smart Ads. Many of the default settings are money wasters.

I recommend you use Expert Mode. Setting up your Google Ads account in Expert Mode is far more complicated than it needs to be, so allow plenty of time and be aware that you may need assistance.

Once you've got your account set up, you can begin to create the advertisements.

You get to choose the search terms (or keywords) for which your advert will appear. For example, if you are a pool cleaning company you'd want to advertise on the keyphrase *pool cleaning*. You may also wish your advert to appear on keywords such as:

- pool filters
- best chlorine for home swimming pools
- how often should I clean my pool

The cost of Google advertising largely depends on the keywords. Here are some examples:

driving school	$0.50
dog wash	$1.80
headaches	$4.00
fix roof	$5.20

The above are in Australian dollars as at the time of writing. These prices will change over time and will differ for other locations.

Google doesn't charge you for when, or how often, your advert is seen. It charges you if, and when, someone clicks on the advert and is taken through to your website.

You would hope that for every 10 clicks to your website, you get a phone call, lead or booking. That being the case, the cost per lead on the search term driving school would be $5, as 10 clicks at 50c each is $5.

Facebook

Most business owners begin their advertising on Facebook by boosting a post. This will rarely get a good return on investment. When you boost a post people who see it might like it, comment on it or share it. Those actions keep them on the Facebook platform – it doesn't take them to your website.

Keeping people on Facebook rarely gets a good return on investment. Getting the person to your website will usually get results. If you want to do Facebook advertising, learn how to create a click-to-website advert.

Small businesses often waste a lot of money on Facebook advertising because they don't have enough knowledge to understand the nuances that can make all the difference between wasted spending and good spending. To hit it out of the ballpark with Facebook advertising you need to know what you are doing. If this is your chosen marketing strategy, seek guidance from the experts or be prepared to put in some hard yards learning the channel.

A small, local business can benefit from a Facebook advertising campaign that has a small spend, but there is a high risk of failure if it's badly implemented. It's often hard for inexperienced players to judge what is bad implementation.

In my experience, Facebook advertising is harder to understand than advertising on Google.

At the time of writing, Facebook has three advertising platforms:

- Ad Center
- Ads Manager
- Business Manager

Facebook tends to draw newbies into Ad Center. Although I don't like all the restrictions in Ad Center, for beginner Facebook advertisers it's much easier than the complicated Ads Manager and therefore I'd recommend it, especially if you struggle with the jargon.

Business Manager is for advertising agencies and you can ignore it.

Ads Manager is frequently more difficult than it sounds. It's not very user friendly once you get there, but it does allow advanced users to optimise the advert much better than the simpler Ad Center. If you're spending a lot of money on Facebook Ads you'll eventually need to graduate to this.

Rather than using keywords, Facebook uses interests. You get to choose which interests or types of people you want to show the advert to. For example, you can choose people who:

- are grandparents
- have a mortgage
- are interested in herbal medicine

and so on – the list is endless.

Each time, as a Facebook user, you click on a post, or 'like' a page that has to do with your interests, that click is noted. All these clicks add up to Facebook knowing a lot about you. And this is how Facebook advertising allows businesses to target people with interests.

The image you choose for your Facebook advert is super important. The image needs to 'stop the scroll.' Nearly everyone who is using Facebook is doing so on a mobile phone. They're scrolling through their newsfeed. For your advert to work, you need to have an image that will stop them scrolling and take notice.

Next Steps – What you can do

Decide if online advertising is the right strategy for your business. If it is, decide between the different options:

» Facebook: product is fun, interesting, quirky or self-indulgent

» Google: product or service is practical, needed or important

» LinkedIn: product is for corporate, multi-nationals or HR

» Instagram: product is suitable for the Instagram generation

» YouTube: product needs explaining as it's revolutionary, new or very different from the usual

If you decide upon online advertising, accept that it's going to be hard to learn.

Use our templates to assist in your preparation.

If you have an agency do it for you, learn enough so you can understand what you are paying for. Ask about the basic packages available, as often agencies will oversell and set up adverts with high monthly administration costs, and it may well be that you don't need that level of sophistication for your business.

Having said that, agencies have experience with a lot of different businesses and industries and they keep up with the latest rules, changes and trends. This experience and knowledge gives them valuable insight.

TEMPLATE
Facebook Advertising

What one product or service are you going to advertise?

What picture are you going to use to 'stop the scroll'?

Is the product or service an easy product or service to understand – not too difficult or not too long lead time? Yes / No

What main interest does the potential buyer have that would indicate their need or desire for the product or service (e.g. homeowner, student, loves cars, musician, grandparent)?

What problem does this product or service solve?

What hurdle does your customer overcome by buying it from you?

What joy do they get from buying from you?

Who are you going to advertise to?
Gender: Age:
Suburb/Town/State:

Headline ideas. 25 characters (including spaces) for each idea

What webpage are you going to get them to click through to?

TEMPLATE
Google Advertising

What <u>one</u> product or service are you going to advertise?

Is this product or service practical or useful to its target audience?
Yes / No

What search terms would the person use on Google that are relevant to this product or service?

What three things are most important about this product or service? 30 characters (including spaces) for each item.

What are two other things that help explain your solution to their problem? 90 characters (including spaces) for each item.

Do you want your phone number to appear in the advert?
Yes / No

Who are you going to advertise to?
Suburb/Town/State:

What webpage are you going to get them to click through to?

Case Study: Physiotherapist — Google Ads

A small, established physiotherapy practice periodically runs Google Ads that are seen only in the suburbs immediately surrounding their location. They recently had their website redesigned so that it was a super mobile-friendly, easy to scroll, one page site.

Henry learnt how to use the platform and create a basic click-to-website advert with the DIY Digital 'Google Ads for beginners' package. He is not running advanced or complicated ads such as re-marketing or display. His practice uses the basic click-to-website advert and chooses its own keywords, suburbs and text.

One beauty of Google Ads (and Facebook Ads) is that you can turn them on and off as you please. And this is what this practice has done.

They tend to run the ad campaign for 5 weeks. They get about 70 clicks to their website with an average cost per click of $3. About 70% of the time, the advert is seen on a mobile phone, meaning that 70% of the people are also seeing their website on a mobile phone. It's just as well they updated their website to be super mobile-friendly!

About 20% of the time the website is viewed on a tablet, with just a small portion (10%) being desktop users. The relatively high tablet use could be associated with an older client base, as older people tend to use tablets more than other age groups.

There's usually a gap of 4 weeks when the advert is not running.

The team has noticed that it often takes 1-3 days at the start of each campaign for bookings to start and then there are significantly more online bookings, especially on Mondays and Tuesdays. There are no other variables in the mix, so they are confident it is the online advertising that is bringing in the new client bookings and, in some cases, older clients coming back.

Case Study: Driving School — Google Ads

Peter owns and manages an established driving school. They run Google Ads, which are seen across the city. They've been using Google Ads for several years, with a gap of about 6 months about a year ago. The gap in advertising has confirmed for Peter that Google Ads has worked for them, as he noticed a decline in new enquiries when they didn't have the ads running.

The website is old-fashioned and has not been updated for many years.

The ads are running continuously every day of the week from 7am-10pm. They spend about $50/month, with an average cost per click of $0.50.

They've added a little extra piece to their Google ad, called a call extension. This is essentially their phone number. The phone number displays 75% of the time and only between the hours of 8am–7pm.

80% of the time the advert is seen on a mobile phone, a low 5% on tablet and the remaining 15% of views are on desktop computers.

They get between 10-15 phone enquiries a week with 4-6 people booking lessons with them. This is enough new clients to keep their business sustainable. If Peter wanted more business, he is confident they could increase their advertising spend to get more enquiries coming in.

CHAPTER 11

ONLINE SHOPS

An online shop, or an e-commerce business, has its own particular requirements in the technology age, over and above service providers.

During my talks with many clients, especially baby boomers, I've sensed from owners of bricks and mortar shops a jealousy, frustration or attitude of being wronged by the introduction of online shopping. Maybe they left it too late, didn't see it as taking on the level of acceptance by customers that it has, or more likely were completely daunted by the technology. Whatever it is, there has been a low level of take-up, by bricks and mortar shops, to go online. Some have successfully transitioned to an online shop or used online to complement their in-store sales, but still today I walk down many main streets viewing the shops and then look them up online only to find they have done very little to give themselves a red hot chance of winning in the online space.

When I talk to these same shop owners, there is a clear and significant misunderstanding of the level of investment and work it takes to get an online shop operational. They've spent so much time working on floor, window and counter displays, payment systems, wholesaler relationships and the myriad of other activities it takes to succeed in the tough retail environment, that another job to do on top of that seems insurmountable.

In addition, online seems so easy. As a buyer you just choose your item, click on a button and it's posted to you. But it's not easy for the owner to create a system for the consumer – there's a lot of hard work behind it.

Whether you are transitioning to an online shop from a bricks and mortar one, using online to complement your in-store sales or starting from scratch, the harsh reality is that getting an online shop up and running takes learning, investment and hard work.

The photos have to be perfect, the descriptions have to be good, the categories and order well considered, the navigation clear and the postage prices must be sorted out.

Many business owners are not aware of the time, attention and money that online shop owners spend on their websites. If they are your competitors, you may be underestimating how much effort they've put in. Online shops can and do succeed, but there are a lot of resources that have gone into them, it's not an easy space to win in.

If you already have a bricks and mortar shop, you already have the relationships with the wholesalers – that's a big plus.

If customers are unable to fully buy your product online, that is, give you their credit card details and have the item posted all in the one online transaction, you are not an e-commerce operation. Many older business owners consider having product photos and descriptions online with a 'send an enquiry' form is sufficient. It's not.

The next biggest mistake is bad photos. Many business owners underestimate how important photos are for the online transaction. Product photos need to be un-cluttered, that is, not have other products or objects in the photo. They need to be in focus, well-lit and look good.

The next biggest mistake is the sense that as long as you have a website with an online shop, that will be sufficient. Customers will find it and buy the products.

The harsh reality (another one) is that there are many e-commerce platforms that are attracting online buyers in droves and they cannot be ignored. Just having one website to sell your products is not enough. Most successful online retailers will have a presence on several channels.

In Australia the big e-commerce channels are:

- eBay
- Amazon
- Gumtree
- Etsy

Not all products are suitable to all platforms, but if your products are, you are doing yourself a big disservice by not selling on them. There's more learning, investment and hard work for the business owner to do.

And we've not even touched on what products to sell!

My main message for this chapter is if you are going online for your products, do it well. Invest time, money, learning and resources. It is unlikely to pay dividends if you do it in a half-baked fashion. Your competitors are beating you – that doesn't mean you can't get a slice of the pie – but you need to make that leap and take the bull by the horns and get on with it. Half-way is not good enough. Go for it – lock, stock and barrel.

Next Steps – What you can do

Take a good, hard look at your online shop. Is the navigation easy to understand? Can customers make a purchase online or is it by enquiry only? Are the photos really stand-out product shots? Is your online shop really good enough? Compare it to your competitors. After that comparison, ask yourself again, is it really good enough?

If it isn't, take a deep breath and make that tough decision. Are you in or are you out?

If you're in – go for it – make your online store the best it possibly can be. Invest lots of time, money, resources and energy – because that's what it will take.

If you're out – get out now – you're possibly sapping your energy, increasing your stress levels and just not enjoying life. There's little to be gained by having a half-hearted attempt at e-commerce which, to you, won't seem half-hearted given you've probably poured hours and hours of frustration into it. But unfortunately, everything has to be close to perfect to keep up with your competitors.

Case Study: Gift Shop — Online Sales

A bricks and mortar gift shop in a small town developed an e-commerce section to their website to sell two of their product ranges online. No advertising, promotion, SEO or online marketing techniques were used beyond local social media and a small amount of email marketing.

In the first year two online orders, on average, were placed a month.

A concerted effort was made to optimise the product pages, using on-page content techniques like those described in the SEO chapter of this book. The next year, after the optimisation was undertaken, the online orders averaged 14 per month.

As would be expected for a gift shop, there was a big spike around Christmas, reaching a peak of 26 orders in December.

As no other online advertising variable was in place, and most orders were first-time customers (i.e. not repeat) and not local to their bricks and mortar shop, the increase in online orders is attributable to the optimisation of the site.

However, an average of 14 orders a month on gift products does not make for a living. And with retail being the tough market it is, in-store sales were also a bit sluggish.

In addition, all the online sales came from one range. The non-performing range was dropped and another range introduced. However, the new range has not picked up the online sales it was hoped they would.

Without a committed and strong online advertising strategy, without selling on the other online platforms, like eBay, without the influencers and without the various other promotional techniques that are used by this business's competitors, will it make it?

Time will tell, but it's not as simple as building it and they will come. That might be true of bridges, but it isn't true of online shops.

EPILOGUE

The Accidental Hero

I often have clients apologise to me because they don't feel they know enough. You know what you know and you don't know what you don't know. All of us are exactly the same in that regard. Why women over 50 (and it seems to be mostly women and mostly those over 50) feel the need to apologise for stuff, I'll never quite know. You're allowed to ask a question without apologising for asking it. You're allowed to say you're not sure about something without apologising for not being sure.

To assist with building your confidence, if this is required, I thought I'd share my own story of failure. As we all have them, and by sharing, it may allow you to feel ok with your not-so-successful outcomes.

Although I give talks on digital marketing, I've mentored business owners in the field and I've now written a book about it, I haven't always known about digital marketing. Like all the others before me, I've had a learning curve. We've all had failures and successes – here's mine. It's about Search Engine Optimisation.

When starting out my business I applied Search Engine Optimisation techniques to my website. Part of this strategy was to write regular articles about digital marketing.

Blog writing, done well, would get lots of people visiting my website.

This is a story about three articles titled:

1. My First Mailchimp Newsletter
2. Facebook Business Page Template
3. Understanding File Size for Images

My First Mailchimp Newsletter

In my business I provide do-it-yourself packages for business owners who want to start email marketing using Mailchimp. So it seemed an obvious choice to write an article about it. This article was written with the clear hope of driving traffic, or visitors, to my website.

Facebook Business Page Template

This article was written to assist people who were already clients of mine to set up a Facebook business page. I wrote this more as an information piece rather than with a marketing outcome in mind. It would be a bonus if the article ranked well on Google searches and new clients found me because of it.

Understanding File Size for Images

This article was only written to assist current clients. I had, and have, many clients who don't understand the basics of image file sizes. Many online platforms, especially websites, have specific requirements for images. Understanding, and then applying these requirements, is a difficult area for many new to it. I did not expect the article to rank well on Google searches and I had no expectations it would increase visitors to my website. I expected the article would only ever be read by clients who I emailed the link to.

How They Rated

How thrilled was I when I googled '*first Mailchimp newsletter*' and it was on page one of a Google search! Just what I was aiming for. A small celebration was afoot in our household.

However, subsequent research on how many people use the search term '*first Mailchimp newsletter*' reveals zero. Nobody uses the search term. I'd written an article without doing the keyword research and without finding out the search volume. Lesson learnt!

I took that lesson to then research how many people search for the term '*Facebook business page*'. As it turns out, oodles do! Lots of people search for this. But alas, my article doesn't get on page one due to the high competition!

The article I didn't expect to rank well on Google searches and I had no expectations it would increase visitors to my website ended up being my accidental hero. The phrase '2mb image' is used a lot in the article on understanding file size for images. Unwittingly it became the keyword. If you google '*2mb image*' you're likely to see the article on page one of your Google search.

It accounts for over 4,000 unique visitors to my website every month – outperforming every other article I've written.

Next time you're struggling with a digital marketing conundrum, please think about my accidental hero. Sometimes you have to learn the hard way.

And with that, I hope this book gives you the ability to learn the easy way, but I suspect there have been some tough lessons leading up to you reading this book and some more tough ones coming your way.

But stick with it – bit by bit – your business success depends on it.

Good luck.
Fiona

> If you've enjoyed this book, please feel free to visit the DIY Digital website at diydigital.com.au. Check out our do-it-yourself packages, free blog articles or sign up for our monthly newsletter.

GLOSSARY

Algorithm: A complicated formula, or equation that online channels like Google and Facebook use. No-one (outside of a few experts in Google/Facebook) really knows what the formula is, although experienced digital marketing specialists learn as much as they can in order to game the system as best they can. The formula can, and does, change frequently. My advice? Don't bother trying to learn it – just accept that it exists.

Avatar: A profile of a pretend person.

Backlink: A link from someone else's website back to your site. If a visitor clicks or taps this link, they will be taken to your website.

Blog: A collection of articles that are written on a website.

Digital Native: Someone who has grown up in the digital age. Born after 1980.

Facebook Ad Center: The simplest area to create Facebook ads.

Facebook Ads Manager: The more complicated area to create Facebook ads.

Facebook Business Manager: The area advertising agencies use to create Facebook ads.

Gif: A short, fun animated image frequently used and shared on social media. They have no sound and play on a continuous loop.

Header: The top of the website where you often see the business logo and business name. Also, page names can be found in the Header, for example Home, About, Services and Contact.

Keyword: The search term people use to find the things they're looking for online. Although it's called a keyword, it's usually 3-5 words and could more accurately be called a keyphrase.

Mailchimp: Simple software available online that allows you to design and send emails in bulk.

Menu: The pages on your website as seen at the top, in the header. For example Home, About, Services and Contact.

Mobile Responsiveness: The ease with which a website performs on different screen sizes, for example, desktops, laptops, tablets and phones.

Organic (Facebook): When used in the context of a discussion about Facebook, and most online channels, organic refers to not paid, i.e. no money has been spent. Therefore, organic posts are information and photos that have been posted for free on your Facebook newsfeed, without boosting them or in other ways paying Facebook to extend their reach.

Organic (Google): When used in the context of a discussion about Google, and most online channels, organic refers to not paid, i.e. no money has been spent. Therefore, websites that show up organically in Google search results have earned their space there without using paid advertising. Google genuinely sees the website as being amongst the best to show the person who is searching the web. This is often, but not always, achieved through Search Engine Optimisation.

Page Speed: How long, in seconds, it takes for a webpage to be displayed fully on the computer or phone screen. The benchmark is for webpages to load in under 3 seconds.

Platform: Sometimes called a channel. Often known by brand name. The following are examples of online marketing platforms: Google, Facebook and Mailchimp. The following are examples of e-commerce platforms: Shopify, WooCommerce and BigCommerce.

Search Engine Optimisation, or SEO: The range of techniques used to get a website found on page one of a Google search.

Search Term: The search term people use to find the things they're looking for online. In other words, the phrase that is typed by people when they're looking for stuff on the computer or phone. A keyword is a search term. They're the same thing.

Smart Ads: The simplest area to create Google ads – but not recommended.

Spam: Sending lots of emails to lots of people who don't want them. Don't do this.

Made in the USA
Monee, IL
04 November 2026

67375703R00105